LAW, CRIME AND LAW ENFORCEMENT

ORGANIZED CRIME: CHALLENGES, TRENDS AND REDUCTION STRATEGIES

LAW, CRIME AND LAW ENFORCEMENT

Additional books in this series can be found on Nova's website
under the Series tab.

Additional E-books in this series can be found on Nova's website
under the E-books tab.

LAW, CRIME AND LAW ENFORCEMENT

ORGANIZED CRIME: CHALLENGES, TRENDS AND REDUCTION STRATEGIES

JASON D. CAMILLERI
EDITOR

Nova Science Publishers, Inc.
New York

For permission to use material from this book please contact us:
Telephone 631-231-7269; Fax 631-231-8175
Web Site: http://www.novapublishers.com

NOTICE TO THE READER

Library of Congress Cataloging-in-Publication Data

Organized crime : challenges, trends and reduction strategies / editor, Jason D. Camilleri.
p. cm.
Includes index.
ISBN 978-1-61324-012-0 (hardcover)
1. Organized crime--United States. 2. Organized crime--United States--Prevention. 3. Transnational crime. 4. Transnational crime--Prevention. I. Camilleri, Jason D.
HV6446.O737 2011
364.1'060973--dc22
2011007510

Published by Nova Science Publishers, Inc. + New York

CONTENTS

PREFACE

Organized crime threatens multiple facets of the United States, including the economy and national security. In fact, the Organized Crime Council was reconvened for the first time in fifteen years to address this continued threat. Organized crime has taken on an increasingly transnational nature, and with more open borders and the expansion of the Internet, criminals endanger the United States not only from within the borders, but beyond. This new book examines issues for Congress concerning whether the resources the federal government allocated to organized crime matters are adequate and appropriately allocated to counter the threats organized crime poses.

Chapter 1- In the last two decades, organized crime has grown more complex, posing evolving challenges for U.S. federal law enforcement. These criminals have transformed their operations in ways that broaden their reach and make it harder for law enforcement to combat them. They have adopted more-networked structural models, internationalized their operations, and grown more tech savvy. They are a significant challenge to U.S. law enforcement.

Chapter 2- Organized crime threatens multiple facets of the United States, including the economy and national security. In fact, the Organized Crime Council was reconvened for the first time in 15 years to address this continued threat. Organized crime has taken on an increasingly transnational nature, and with more open borders and the expansion of the Internet, criminals endanger the United States not only from within the borders, but beyond. Threats come from a variety of criminal organizations, including Russian, Asian, Italian, Balkan, Middle Eastern, and African syndicates. Policymakers may question whether the tools they have provided the federal government to combat organized crime are still effective for countering today's evolving risks.

Chapter 3- In January of 2010, the International Center of the National Institute of Justice (NIJ) assembled international experts and practitioners to assess the state of research on international organized crime (IOC). Two recent developments made this an opportune time for a working group to engage in a robust and critical reflection. The first was an expansion of IOC research. Although the number of books, journal articles and reports on IOC have steadily increased in recent years, the ways IOC research has expanded in other ways made this a good time to call such a meeting. For example, IOC research now goes beyond the traditional disciplines of criminology and sociology to include anthropology, economics, political science, history and other academic disciplines. Moreover, scholarly examination of IOC has gone beyond description and has increasingly focused on critical issues, such as how to improve the scientific rigor of IOC research. Last, this research now uses a mixture of methodologies, including historical, experimental, quantitative, qualitative and case study designs and increasingly implements international or comparative research designs to expand the geographical breadth of studies.

Chapter 4- In recent years, international organized crime has expanded considerably in presence, sophistication and significance – and it now threatens many aspects of how Americans live, work and do business. International organized crime promotes corruption, violence and other illegal activities, jeopardizes our border security, and causes human misery. It undermines the integrity of our banking and financial systems, commodities and securities markets, and our cyberspace. In short, international organized crime is a national security problem that demands a strategic, targeted and concerted U.S. Government response.

In: Organized Crime
Editor: Jason D. Camilleri

ISBN: 978-1-61324-012-0

Chapter 1

ORGANIZED CRIME: AN EVOLVING CHALLENGE FOR U.S. LAW ENFORCEMENT*

Jerome P. Bjelopera and Kristin M. Finklea

SUMMARY

In the last two decades, organized crime has grown more complex, posing evolving challenges for U.S. federal law enforcement. These criminals have transformed their operations in ways that broaden their reach and make it harder for law enforcement to combat them. They have adopted more-networked structural models, internationalized their operations, and grown more tech savvy. They are a significant challenge to U.S. law enforcement.

Modern organized criminals often prefer cellular or networked structural models for their flexibility and avoid the hierarchies that previously governed more traditional organized crime groups such as the Cosa Nostra. Fluid network structures make it harder for law enforcement to infiltrate, disrupt, and dismantle conspiracies. Many 21st century organized crime groups opportunistically form around specific, short-term schemes and may outsource portions of their operations rather than keeping it all "in-house."

---

* This is an edited, reformatted and augmented version of a Congressional Research Services publication, dated December 23, 2010.

Globalization has revolutionized both licit and illicit commerce. Commercial and technological innovations have reduced national trade barriers, widened transportation infrastructure, and bolstered volumes of international business. The Internet and extensive cellular telephone networks have fostered rapid communication. Integrated financial systems, which allow for easy global movement of money, are exploited by criminals to launder their illicit proceeds. Estimates suggest that money laundering annually accounts for between 2% and 5% of world GDP. Simultaneously, borders are opportunities for criminals and impediments to law enforcement.

Organized criminals have expanded their technological "toolkits," incorporating technology-driven fraud into their capabilities. Their operations can harm U.S. citizens without ever having a physical presence in the country. These illicit activities include cyber intrusions into corporate databases, theft of individual consumer credit card information, fencing of stolen merchandise online, and leveraging technology to aid in narcotics smuggling. Further, criminal organizations —which have historically burrowed into and exploited local ethnic communities—can now rely on Internet connectivity and extensive, international transportation linkages to target localities around the globe.

Since the terrorist attacks of September 11, 2001, there has been a shift in law enforcement attention and resources toward counterterrorism-related activities and away from traditional crime fighting activities including the investigation of organized crime. Although the effects of organized crime may not be seen in a consolidated attack resulting in the physical loss of life, they are far-reaching—impacting economic stability, public health and safety, as well as national security. One challenge facing law enforcement is that the federal investigation of organized crime matters has not historically been a centralized effort, and there is no single agency charged with investigating organized crime in the way the Federal Bureau of Investigation (FBI) has been designated the lead investigative agency for terrorism. Further, resources to tackle this issue are divided among federal agencies and little consensus exists regarding the scope of the problem, the measurable harm caused by these groups, or how to tackle them. As such, Congress may exert oversight regarding the federal coordination of organized crime investigations. Policymakers may also debate the efficacy of current resources appropriated to combat organized crime.

INTRODUCTION

In the last two decades, organized crime has grown more complex, posing evolving challenges for U.S. federal law enforcement. This is largely because these criminals have transformed their operations in ways that broaden their reach and make it harder for law enforcement to define and combat the threat they pose. Globalization and technological innovation have not only impacted legitimate commerce, but they have simultaneously revolutionized crime. In response to these forces, organized criminals have adopted more-networked structural models, internationalized their operations, and grown more tech savvy. Criminals have become more elusive as the illicit world rapidly evolves in response to these changes. Meanwhile, law enforcement "plays by yesterday's rules and increasingly risks dealing only with the weakest criminals and the easiest problems," according to the Strategic Alliance Group, a partnership of seven law enforcement agencies from five nations.[1] Organized criminals see international borders as opportunities while law enforcement views them as obstacles. Criminals have expanded their range of tools and targets as well.

Potentially compounding matters, there is no clear definition at the federal level of what constitutes organized crime, which can make it difficult to measure the scope of this problem and devise a cohesive federal response. There also appears to be a fragmentation of efforts among federal agencies charged with combating organized crime itself or issues related to it, such as drug trafficking, copyright violation, cybercrime, human trafficking, and health care fraud. Further complicating all of this, since the terrorist attacks of September 11, 2001 (9/11), there has been a shift in law enforcement attention and resources more toward counterterrorism-related activities and away from traditional crime fighting activities—including the investigation of organized crime.

Motivated by money, organized crime fills needs not met by licit market structures and/or exploits businesses, consumers, and nations for profit. Organized criminals have capitalized on commercial and technological advances that have bolstered communication and international business. They use innovative methods of moving illegal proceeds around the world. Some nations have also witnessed the creation of ties between powerful business figures, politicians, and criminals.

Modern organized criminals may prefer cellular or networked structural models for their flexibility and avoid the hierarchies governed by elaborate initiation rituals that were favored by their predecessors. Fluid network structures make it harder for law enforcement to infiltrate, disrupt, and dismantle conspiracies. Many 21st century organized crime groups opportunistically form around specific, short-term schemes. Further, these groups may outsource portions of their operations rather than keeping all of their expertise "in-house."

This report provides an analysis of how organized crime has capitalized on globalization by using borders as opportunities, relying on fast-paced technological change, and adapting its organizational structures. It illustrates how these transformations can impact U.S. persons, businesses, and interests. The report includes a discussion of how U.S. law enforcement conceptualizes organized crime in the 21st century and concludes by examining potential issues for Congress, including the extent to which organized crime is a national security threat (partly to be tackled by U.S. law enforcement agencies), congressional oversight regarding the federal coordination of organized crime investigations, and the utility of current resources appropriated to combat organized crime.

Conceptualizing Organized Crime

One of the primary challenges in conceptualizing organized crime is that it is usually not thought of as a specific crime, but rather as a large number of illicit activities committed by groups of individuals who are often so loosely connected that the members themselves do not know who their criminal associates may be. This inherently leads to a lack of consistency in the way different groups—scholars, policymakers, various federal law enforcement agencies, and nation states—view what constitutes organized crime and think about how to combat it. The inconsistent conceptualization of organized crime also makes it difficult to measure its impact. Without a clear indication of what constitutes organized crime, analysts face methodological and conceptual problems in estimating the harm it causes.[2]

Agency Definitions

In April 2008, the Department of Justice (DOJ) released its *Overview of the Law Enforcement Strategy to Combat International Organized Crime* (*Overview*). The document included an expansive definition of international organized crime as

> self-perpetuating associations of individuals who operate internationally for the purpose of obtaining power, influence, monetary

> and/or commercial gains, wholly or in part by illegal means, while protecting their activities through a pattern of corruption and/or violence. There is no single structure under which international organized criminals operate; they vary from hierarchies to clans, networks and cells, and may evolve to other structures. The crimes they commit also vary. International organized criminals act conspiratorially in their criminal activities and possess certain characteristics which may include, but are not limited to:
>
> a. In at least part of their activities they commit violence or other acts which are likely to intimidate, or make actual or implicit threats to do so;
> b. They exploit differences between countries to further their objectives, enriching their organization, expanding its power, and/or avoiding detection and apprehension;
> c. They attempt to gain influence in government, politics and commerce through corrupt as well as legitimate means;
> d. They have economic gain as their primary goal, not only from patently illegal activities but also from investment in legitimate business; and
> e. They attempt to insulate both their leadership and membership from detection, sanction, and/or prosecution through their organizational structure.[3]

The definition was formulated for the purposes of the strategy and clearly focuses on international criminal organizations, but it suggests key principles undergirding DOJ's understanding of organized crime, which shares self-perpetuating structure, illegal profit as a motive, violence/intimidation, and corruption as key techniques. DOJ states in its *Overview* that the definition can encompass drug trafficking organizations and street gangs, even though the groups are not the focus of the strategy.[4] Further, the definition of international organized crime in the document was not necessarily created for purposes outside this strategy.

The Federal Bureau of Investigation (FBI) has a similar, if shorter, definition of organized crime. Unlike DOJ's *Overview,* the FBI's definition is not limited to international groups:

> The FBI defines organized crime as any group having some manner of a formalized structure and whose primary objective is to obtain money through illegal activities. Such groups maintain their position through the use of actual or threatened violence, corrupt public officials, graft, or

extortion, and generally have a significant impact on the people in their locales, region, or the country as a whole.[5]

This definition's breadth is tempered by the ethnic or geographic focus applied to the FBI's organized crime programs. It appears that the FBI's conceptualization of organized crime emphasizes a criminal group's ethnicity or geographic origins. The agency divides its Organized Crime Section based at headquarters into three Units, and the FBI prioritizes its organized crime cases based on these ethno-geographic groupings:[6] (1) the Cosa Nostra,[7] Italian organized crime, and racketeering; (2) Eurasian/Middle Eastern organized crime; and (3) Asian and African criminal enterprises.[8]

Hazy Boundaries

These agency definitions hold little sway over what is practically investigated as "organized crime" by federal agencies. For example, FBI and the Drug Enforcement Administration (DEA)—both DOJ components—investigate activities and groups that can be viewed as "organized crime" but are not conventionally conceived as such—rendering the concept of organized crime rather hazy. Although its definition of organized crime potentially encompasses all crimes committed by structured groups for profit, the FBI does not investigate or view drug trafficking organizations (DTOs) as "organized crime," even though many DTOs exhibit a high degree of internal structure and not only traffic in illegal drugs but are involved in human and weapons smuggling, money laundering, extortion, kidnappings for ransom, and murder, among other crimes. Even the geographic or ethnic focus of Mexican or Colombian DTOs does not qualify them as organized crime for the FBI. The agency also distinguishes gangs from organized crime.

Similarly, the DEA investigates DTOs but not organized crime in general. Yet, DEA and Bureau of Alcohol, Tobacco, Firearms, and Explosives (ATF) representatives have referred to Mexican DTOs as the "greatest organized crime threat to the United States."[9] Also, the DEA spearheads the Organized Crime Drug Enforcement Task Force (OCDETF) Program, which targets—with the intent to disrupt and dismantle—major drug trafficking and money laundering organizations.[10] DTOs are the primary focus of OCDETF operations while other major organized crime groups that focus on a range of crimes other than drug trafficking, and are engaged in significant money laundering activities, are not leading targets of OCDETF investigations.

Structured groups engaged in activities such as health care fraud, cyber intrusions, identity theft, mass marketing fraud, copyright violations, human trafficking, and alien smuggling are not necessarily viewed as organized criminals by U.S. federal agencies. In fact, investigative programs within the federal government have been developed to combat each of these individual criminal activities without specifically characterizing them as "organized crime." However, groups committing such illicit deeds can easily fit under most definitions of organized crime, especially if they engage in violence, threats of violence, or corruption alongside their other illegal activities.

Not only is there a disconnect between the definition and investigation of organized crime among federal agencies, but this disconnect exists with respect to the prosecution of organized crime cases as well. Organized crime, DTOs, and gangs are prosecuted separately, through the Organized Crime and Racketeering Section (OCRS), the Narcotic and Dangerous Drug Section (NDDS), and the Gang Unit, respectively. DOJ has indicated, however, that although drug trafficking organizations and gangs are not considered part of international organized crime for program purposes, they are indeed organized crime threats.[11] Also, citing similarities in the prosecution of organized crime and gang cases, DOJ has announced consolidation of OCRS; the Criminal Division's Gang Unit; and the National Gang Targeting, Enforcement, and Coordination Center (GangTECC) into a single Organized Crime and Gang Section.[12] However, this consolidation will not include the prosecution of DTOs. DOJ may continue, at some point in the future, to harmonize its policies regarding organized crime groups, DTOs, and gangs in order to place DOJ more in line with its international partners. This alignment may further aid in multilateral investigations and prosecutions of transnational criminal organizations. For instance, some nations, such as Mexico, have defined organized crime as including drug trafficking organizations.[13] Further, the United Nations (UN), through the United Nations Convention Against Transnational Organized Crime, has defined a transnational organized criminal group as

> a structured group of three or more persons, existing for a period of time and acting in concert with the aim of committing one or more serious crimes or offenses established in accordance with this Convention [the United Nations Convention Against Transnational Organized Crime], in order to obtain, directly or indirectly, a financial or other material benefit.[14]

Of note, the UN definition of organized crime presents a view of organized crime as having an adaptable structure rather than the rigid hierarchical structure that previously governed more-traditional organized crime groups such as the Cosa Nostra.

As illustrated in **Figure 1**, a federal, policy-driving definition of organized crime may be helpful in clarifying the roles of U.S. law enforcement agencies in combating this threat. Such a definition could help clarify the (1) harm imposed by organized crime, (2) federal resources dedicated to combating it, (3) federal agencies responsible for fighting it, and (4) extent to which organized crime poses both public and national security threats to the United States. Currently, the federal government does not appear to have a clear definition of organized crime. Therefore, it may be more difficult for policymakers to exercise both legislative and oversight responsibilities in order to bolster the federal government's abilities to counter organized crime.

Statutory Definition

There is no current statutory definition of organized crime. The Omnibus Crime Control and Safe Streets Act of 1968, as amended (P.L. 90-351),[15] had at one point defined organized crime as "the unlawful activities of the members of a highly organized, disciplined association engaged in supplying illegal goods and services, including but not limited to gambling, prostitution, loan sharking, narcotics, labor racketeering, and other unlawful activities of members of such organizations." This definition—repealed in the Justice System Improvement Act of 1979 (P.L. 96-157)—appears to be even broader than DOJ's or the FBI's conceptualizations. Similarly, in the Racketeer Influenced and Corrupt Organizations (RICO)[16] provisions, organized crime is described in terms of an "enterprise" and a "pattern of racketeering activity."[17] The predicate offenses for racketeering include a host of state and federal crimes listed in 18 U.S.C. § 1961.

Although RICO does not define organized crime, it provides a definition for an "enterprise." It does not, however, describe those attributes of a *criminal* enterprise that distinguish it from a legal enterprise. In addition, this provision describes organized crime more in terms of the illegal activities committed by conspirators rather than in terms of the criminal organization. As such, these statutory provisions could encompass the activities of not only organized crime groups but of terrorist groups and corrupt businesses as well. Largely describing organized crime as a list of crimes may help in the effective prosecution of these groups, but it provides little aid in developing an understanding of the groups themselves.[18] Moreover, the statutory provisions offer limited guidance regarding criminal organizations and the nature of their operational structure.

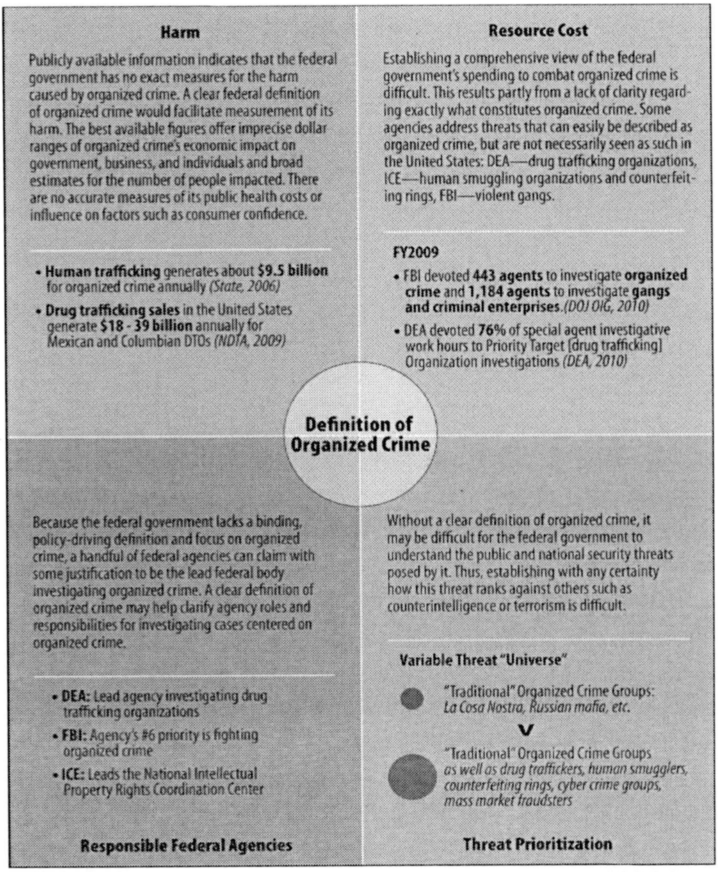

Source: U.S. Department of State, *Trafficking In Persons Report 2006*, June 2006, p. 13, http://www.state.gov/ documents/organization/66086.pdf; U.S. Department of Justice, National Drug Intelligence Center, *National Drug Threat Assessment 2009,* Product No. 2008-Q0317-005, December 2008, p. 9, http://www.usdoj.gov/ndic/pubs31/31379/31379p.pdf; U.S. Department of Justice, Office of the Inspector General, *Follow-up Audit of Federal Bureau of Investigation Personnel Resource Management and Casework*, Audit Report 10-24, April 2010, p. 52, http://www.justice.gov/oig/reports/FBI U.S. Department of Justice, Drug Enforcement Administration, *FY2011 Performance Budget*, Congressional Budget Submission, pp. 50, 52, http://www.justice.gov/jmd/2011justification/pdf/fy11-dea-justification.pdf. Graphic created by CRS Graphics.

Figure 1. Definition of Organized Crime: An Issue for Federal Policy.

This report applies much of the UN definition of organized crime in its narrative discussion of criminal activity. In other words, the analysis includes groups engaged in sustained criminal enterprises, such as—but not limited to—drug traffickers, mafia families, smugglers, violent gangs, and fraudsters. These operations may or may not have an international dimension to them (which is a requirement under the guidelines of DOJ's "Overview of the Law Enforcement Strategy to Combat International Organized Crime"), but they directly impact U.S. persons, businesses, and/or interests. While this conceptualization is broader than the definitions of organized crime used by U.S. law enforcement agencies, it incorporates a range of criminality that may inform Congress in future legislation impacting organized crime. The cases and examples discussed in this report are not intended to set definitional boundaries for organized crime.

ORGANIZED CRIME ADAPTING TO GLOBALIZATION

Organized crime targeting the United States has internationalized and its structures have flattened. The popular image of mobsters employing elaborate initiation rituals and strict codes of conduct to control crews that assail their own communities is outmoded. Today, nimble, adaptive, loosely structured small groups with global reach harm consumers, businesses, and government interests on a daily basis. Commercial and technological innovations are behind this transformation. They have helped to reduce national trade barriers, widen transportation infrastructure, and bolster volumes of international business. Smugglers have taken advantage of growing international commerce to hide illicit trade. The Internet and extensive cellular telephone networks have fostered rapid communication, simultaneously revolutionizing licit and illicit commerce. For example, integrated financial systems allow for easy global movement of money. Estimates suggest that money laundering annually accounts for between 2% and 5% of world GDP.[19] Criminal organizations targeting the United States operate in many of the world's nations. Areas wracked by social disorder, inadequate policing, and poor governance offer opportunities for organized crime to take root.[20] These groups exploit diaspora communities in the United States as cover for their operations, situating elements of their global operations among immigrant enclaves.

Organized crime groups are becoming more entrepreneurial or market focused, reacting to changes in both illicit and licit economies.[21] Of course, they are still heavily involved in activities such as narcotics trafficking and money laundering (which have been greatly impacted by globalization), but organized criminals are increasingly involved in less "traditional" high-tech operations encompassing identity theft, counterfeiting of goods, and various types of fraud.

Borders as Opportunity

Modern organized criminals prey upon weaknesses in international transportation and customs security regimens.[22] And border policing efforts struggle to keep pace with the expansion of international commerce. Specialized criminal networks smuggle items such as narcotics, counterfeit goods, stolen goods, and bulk cash, as well as humans, around the world and into the United States. They hide their contraband within the growing volume of legitimate global trade. Prior to the global recession, between 1995 and 2008 the volume of global containerized traffic tripled.[23] Drug traffickers move large loads of cocaine, eventually destined for U.S. markets, from South America to Mexico via containerized shipping. International counterfeiters use containers to smuggle their fake goods into the United States. As Moisės Naím has succinctly put it, most illicit trade involves copycats, smugglers, and traffickers.[24] While individuals can and do engage in these activities, a good deal can be attributed to organized crime.

Copycats and Smugglers

Criminal groups engage in counterfeiting and smuggling across and within the borders of the United States. This activity includes a wide range of products and influences the lives of everyday Americans, U.S. businesses, and government.

Counterfeiting and Piracy

Counterfeiting highlights the nexus between globalization and the modernization of organized crime. Although it is difficult, if not impossible, to determine how deeply immersed organized criminals are in this activity, at least one study has suggested serious involvement.[25] Further, in a recent speech before the International Intellectual Property Summit, Attorney General Holder reinforced the need for the international law enforcement community to combat "the international networks of organized criminals now seeking to profit from IP [intellectual property] crimes."[26] In areas such as film piracy, counterfeiting does not necessarily involve high entry costs or large legal penalties when compared to more conventional criminal activity such as drug trafficking.[27] It is also potentially very lucrative. With little infrastructure—a high-speed Internet connection, scanner, and copier and off-the-shelf software—criminals around the globe can easily imitate the branding and packaging that accompanies products, let alone copy the products themselves.[28] Counterfeiting and pirating goods[29] involves the violation of intellectual property rights (IPR),[30] essential to creative and high-tech industries particularly reliant on copyrights, trademarks, and patents to protect innovation. Counterfeiting and piracy potentially harm legitimate businesses and consumers, sapping profits and brand value and flooding markets with inferior and even dangerous products masquerading as legitimate goods. Aside from enforcement outlays, the activity also costs governments tax revenue and may slow economic growth by driving down incentives to innovate.[31]

Between FY2005 and FY2008, the yearly domestic value[32] of IPR-related law enforcement seizures of contraband in the United States leaped from $93 million to $273 million. In FY2009, the domestic value of seizures dropped 4%.[33] This is likely due to the global recession. Products originating in China—both Mainland China and Hong Kong—accounted for over 85% of these IPR seizures in FY2008 and FY2009.[34] Two 2010 operations in the United States together netted $240 million in counterfeit materials. The hauls included fake Rolex watches, Coach handbags, pirated DVDs, and fake pharmaceutical products. Much of the material came from China.[35]

Auto Theft Rings

Another example of organized criminals viewing borders as opportunity involves auto theft. Although international automobile theft has existed almost as long as cars have been around,[36] the integration of worldwide markets and expansion of international shipping have greatly impacted it by facilitating international transport of stolen automobiles. Assessing the level of such activity is very difficult since few metrics for it exist. Regardless, today's international automobile theft rings benefit from the high levels of cargo container traffic ushered in by globalization. These groups profit by stealing vehicles in the United States and shipping them abroad, where they are sold. Such illicit operations react to global demand for luxury vehicles, and in some instances are extremely responsive to market forces. They trawl large U.S. metropolitan areas that have assortments of vehicles and rely on rail or port facilities to move stolen vehicles abroad.[37]

In June 2010, law enforcement officials announced indictments of 17 participants in an alleged scheme that pilfered 450 cars annually in New York, New Jersey, and Connecticut. According to law enforcement officials, the group, described as a "steal to order" outfit by New York State Attorney General Andrew Cuomo, filled specific requests from U.S. customers and others in Senegal and netted up to $25,000 per car. The group supposedly relied on specialists who could reprogram car keys to match a vehicle's specific code, exporters, and two car dealership employees, among others. The ring allegedly stored vehicles in four Bronx, NY, garages and loaded those destined for Senegal into shipping containers, concealing the cars behind furniture.[38]

Human Smuggling and Trafficking

Criminal organizations are taking advantage of an unprecedented era of international migration, including illegal migration to the United States.[39] However, since 2007 illegal immigration to the United States has declined.[40] This may be attributable, in part, to dwindling job opportunities resulting from the global recession and increased immigration enforcement activity along the U.S. Southwest border.[41] Nonetheless, criminal organizations continue to capitalize on the desire of unauthorized immigrants to enter the United States. Networks of human smugglers and others— including Mexican drug trafficking organizations (DTOs) that have broadened their money-generating activities to include human and weapon smuggling, counterfeiting, kidnapping for ransom, and extortion—bring unauthorized immigrants across the border and into the United States.[42] In one well-known case, Cheng Chui Ping—also known as "Sister Ping"—sentenced in March 2006, had led an international human smuggling ring that was responsible for smuggling Chinese villagers to the United States between the early 1980s and April 2000. In a 2006 press release, DOJ described her as "one of the first, and ultimately most successful, alien smugglers of all time."[43] At the start, Ping's smuggling ring brought small numbers of villagers to the United States via aircraft, using fake immigration documents. She turned from exclusive reliance on air transit to include the use of maritime shipping as her operation matured. This way, Ping likely exploited increasing volumes of international seaborne cargo engendered by globalization to mask her illegal movement of human beings. She eventually developed the capability to smuggle hundreds of victims at a time via cargo ships, where the villagers could be stashed below the deck until they reached their U.S. destination and eventually paid her exorbitant smuggling fees.[44] Criminals who smuggle individuals into the United States may also turn the smuggling into a trafficking situation by increasing the immigrants' debts owed once they have been smuggled to the United States. The smugglers/traffickers may then require their victims to work for a period of time to pay off the debts.[45]

Organized crime exploits individuals through both labor and sex trafficking. In 2006, the FBI reported that human trafficking generates about $9.5 billion for organized crime annually.[46] However, as the Government Accountability Office (GAO) has noted, estimates regarding the global scale of human trafficking are questionable;[47] as such, any estimates regarding the proceeds generated through these crimes may not be representative of their true scope. These criminal organizations target both U.S. citizens and foreign nationals who are drawn to visions of better lives in the United States.

International borders often play a central role in the dynamics involved in forced labor and sex trafficking. In many instances, victims likely perceive borders and border security regimens as insurmountable barriers via legitimate means, requiring them to turn to illicit methods of transit offered by traffickers. Organized criminals prey on victims' powerful desires to live or work in other countries. While the following two cases may not have been prosecuted by DOJ as traditional "organized crime," the networks involved highlight some of the dynamics involved in labor and sex trafficking. In August 2010, federal law enforcement announced an indictment of six individuals for participation in an alleged conspiracy to exploit Thai nationals through forced labor in the United States. The defendants allegedly enticed workers to the United States by offering opportunities for lucrative jobs. Once in the United States, the approximately 400 Thai workers had their passports confiscated, were threatened with economic harm and deportation, and were forced to work on farms in Washington and Hawaii.[48] In another case, four individuals from the United States, Mexico, and Guatemala were sentenced in April 2010 for involvement in a sex trafficking organization that targeted young Mexican women. They lured these women to the United States on the promise of better lives or legitimate employment. Once the women were brought to the United States, they were instead physically threatened, beaten, intimidated, and forced to engage in commercial sex.[49] DOJ has also reported an uptick in Asian organized crime groups becoming involved as pimps or brokers in domestic human sex trafficking. Although the increase is noted for Asian organized crime groups, involvement in sex trafficking is certainly not limited by ethnic or geographic origin; these criminals collaborate with other, non-Asian groups to further their sex trafficking enterprises.[50]

Drug Trafficking

In the last decade, cocaine has become a truly global commodity dependent on illicit market fluctuations. Traffickers now can leverage wide, international distribution networks to ride out pressures or changes that may make their traditional illicit markets less hospitable. According to media reports, some Colombian and Mexican cocaine suppliers have shifted sizeable amounts of product using containerized shipping—hiding their illicit material within the daily globalized flow of legitimate seaborne international commerce.[51] And some of the Mexican Gulf Cartel's smuggling activity involving European markets has used the United States as a transshipment point.[52]

When it comes to the internationalization of cocaine markets, not all the news involves the growth of supply, however. Global demand for cocaine has partly impacted U.S. bound supplies of the drug. Cocaine availability levels in the United States have decreased since 2006. Diversion of cocaine to European and Latin American markets by Colombian and Mexican drug cartels has fueled this downturn in availability, as have coca eradication efforts, large seizures, law enforcement pressure on Mexican cartels, and violent inter-cartel rivalries.[53]

While the story of globalized drug smuggling impacting the United States often revolves around Colombian and Mexican cartels specializing in drugs such as cocaine, marijuana, heroin, and methamphetamine, criminal groups trafficking narcotics come in all sizes and handle a variety of drugs. Because of the ease of international communications, travel, and transportation networks inherent in globalization, drug trafficking groups need not be directly tied to the large cartels to have significant worldwide reach. Even relatively small groups can forge far-flung supply and transportation links.

The FBI's operation Black Eagle tracked a small Albanian network of alleged criminals based in northern New Jersey who were indicted in March 2009.[54] The network purportedly had domestic ties to Chicago, Detroit, and Texas, as well as international links to Macedonia and Albania. At one point, the group of opportunists supposedly conspired to smuggle 100 kilograms of heroin from Albania to the United States. According to the FBI, the group planned to use a Balkan front company to conceal the heroin in containerized shipments of furniture bound for the United States. The heroin was purportedly to come from Afghanistan, likely via Turkey and into Albania. There was no clear cut leadership in the loosely knit group. The heroin deal was going to be one last score before some of the criminals "retired," according to the FBI. They were also likely involved with stealing and selling pharmaceuticals, illegal gambling, dealing ecstasy, and theft of retail goods.[55]

In another case involving a relatively small group, Phuong Thi Tran pleaded guilty in February 2010 for her involvement in what has been described in press reports as an Asian drug trafficking ring that smuggled ecstasy pills and other drugs into the United States from Canada, where they were manufactured. Tran, who lived in Canada, is originally from Vietnam and served as the group's ringleader. She oversaw an operation that smuggled millions of ecstasy pills into the United States between 2002 and 2008, when she was arrested.[56]

Money Laundering

Making ill-gotten gains appear legitimate is critical to the success of organized criminals. For many criminals, the movement of money—either as bulk cash or digital transactions—across international borders plays an integral role in this process. They use many techniques to launder money, often exploiting legitimate financial structures to mask the illegal origins of their profits. Money laundering includes three fundamental steps: (1) placement, the introduction of illicit funds into licit financial systems; (2) layering, the movement (often international) of illicit funds through a variety of business structures to obscure its origins; and (3) integration, the use of illicit funds that at this stage appear legitimate in lawful business transactions.[57] It is impossible to determine with any accuracy how much money is laundered by organized criminals whose operations impact the United States. However, U.S. government estimates suggest that Mexican and Columbian drug trafficking organizations earn between $18 billion and $39 billion annually from sales in the United States.[58] Annually, perhaps between $20 billion and $25 billion in bank notes is smuggled across the Southwest border into Mexico.[59] How much of this is profit and then laundered is unclear.[60] While bulk cash smuggling is an important means by which criminals move illegal profits from the United States into Mexico, they have increasingly turned to stored-value cards[61] to move money. With these cards, criminals are able to avoid the reporting requirement under which they would have to declare any amount over $10,000 in cash moving across the border.[62] Aside from bulk cash smuggling and stored-value cards, Mexican traffickers move and launder money by using digital currency accounts, e-businesses that facilitate money transfers via the Internet, online role-playing games or virtual worlds that enable the exchange of game-based currencies for real currency, and "mobile payments through cell phones that provide traffickers with remote access to existing payment mechanisms such as bank and credit card accounts and prepaid cards."[63]

Organized criminals also use the globalized international financial system in the layering stage of money laundering. The United States is impacted by this from at least two directions. Criminals operating abroad can exploit U.S. structures to launder money while those operating domestically can wash their illicit profits abroad in an attempt to avoid U.S. law enforcement. Large financial markets such as New York, where criminal activity is potentially hidden within voluminous legitimate business, are used by criminals. Criminals use banks and businesses to launder money in offshore locations with strict privacy laws such as Panama, the Cayman Islands, or the Isle of Man. In these locales, law enforcement struggles to determine the true ownership of assets.[64]

International or domestic shell companies can be used for money laundering. They are legal entities that have no independent operations or assets of their own and largely exist only on paper. Shell companies have legitimate purposes, for example, "they may be formed to obtain financing prior to starting operations."[65] Regardless, DOJ has identified U.S.-based shell companies as especially difficult to investigate because "lax company formation laws [allow] criminals [to] form [them] quickly and cheaply and obtain virtual anonymity."[66]

Organized criminals likely rely on the veneer of legitimacy conferred by U.S.-based shell companies, which in many instances allow criminals to conceal their ownership.[67] Most U.S. states do not require owner information when companies are formed or even on annual or biennial reports.[68] Individuals can distance themselves from the actual formation of specific shell companies by using company formation agents (registered agents) to establish them. Shell companies enable criminals to move money around the globe through legitimate bank accounts without attracting law enforcement scrutiny. With relative ease, a criminal organization can open multiple shell companies worldwide and systematically distance ill-gotten gains from their criminal origins, leaving behind a hard-to-untangle web of accounts, legitimate corporations, and transactions.[69] Both Mexico's Sinaloa Cartel and alleged Eurasian organized crime figure Semion Mogilevich have likely used U.S. shell companies to launder money.[70]

ORGANIZED CRIME AND TECHNOLOGICAL CHANGE

Organized criminals have expanded their technological "toolkits." They have adapted to incorporate technology-driven fraud into their capabilities.[71] Their operations can harm U.S. citizens without ever having a physical presence in the country. Organized crime groups engage in a wide variety of tech savvy mass marketing frauds. Even traditional arenas of criminal activity such as illegal gambling have been transformed by the Internet. For example, illegal gambling has been a staple in the Cosa Nostra's criminal diet for decades. In recent years, they have branched out into Internet gambling,[72] which debuted in the mid 1990s.[73] Operation Heat, an investigation by the New Jersey Division of Criminal Justice, led to the arrest of Brian Cohen, who allegedly facilitated the Lucchese family's offshore gambling activities. According to law enforcement officials, the family earned billions of dollars via offshore Internet activity that included a website and a Costa Rican wire room that handled transactions, both managed by Cohen.[74]

Mass Marketing Fraud

The International Mass-Marketing Fraud Working Group defines mass marketing fraud as

> Fraud schemes that use mass-communications media—including telephones, the Internet, mass mailings, television, radio, and even personal contact—to contact, solicit, and obtain money, funds, or other items of value from multiple victims in one or more jurisdictions.[75]

Mass marketing fraud involves a wide range of criminal activity that has been transformed by globalization and technological change. It can be perpetrated by individuals, small groups, or sophisticated criminal enterprises. Parsing out exactly how much of this activity can be attributed to organized criminals is tricky, but experts suggest that "fraudulent mass marketing operations are increasingly transnational, interconnected, and fluid."[76] "Boiler room" scams, one iteration of the fraud with a long history, entail groups of fraudsters making high-pressure deceptive merchandise pitches and misleading service offers to unwitting customers around the world. Recently, criminals have innovated based on tried-and-true boiler room schemes by outsourcing some activity to specialists, internationalizing their operations, and adopting sophisticated concealment strategies for their communications capabilities and locations.

The Cosa Nostra and other organized criminals use boiler rooms.[77] In June 2010, the FBI raided an alleged boiler room operation involving Anthony Guarino, a purported Bonnano family soldier. According to law enforcement officials, the boiler room hoodwinked elderly investors into buying shares of companies, and 40% of the money taken in was handed over to the boiler room operators as commissions.[78]

Technology Transforms Advance Fee Fraud (AFF)

Since the 1970s, technological advancements have revolutionized advance fee fraud (AFF) operations—a form of mass marketing fraud used by criminal organizations and individual fraudsters. Today, these schemes often involve criminals appealing for money via unsolicited (spam) emails. These emails typically request an initial cash payment from recipients. The initial cash payment supposedly facilitates the disbursement of a much larger sum of money to the email recipients.[79] The later sum never arrives. A recent AFF email scam attempting to dupe people into believing they had been contacted by the FBI's Detroit Field Office asked email recipients to forward $14,300 in return for the release of over $18 million to their accounts. In one of the emails associated with this scheme, the fraudsters suggest that "the International clamp down on Terrorist [sic]" has frozen the larger pot of money.[80]

Also known as "419 scams" after a section in the Nigerian criminal code, the broad outlines of the modern version of AFF originated in Nigeria during the 1970s and early 1980s, and perhaps even earlier. AFF's original incarnation may stretch back to the 1500s in the "Spanish Prisoner" scheme. Wealthy English business owners were asked to help pay for a rescue mission to save someone held captive in Spain. In return, they would supposedly receive part of the vast alleged reward payment. Of course, it never came.[81] In the late 1970s and early 1980s, Nigerian fraudsters became known for mailing unsolicited letters requesting monetary assistance in transferring frozen or hidden funds out of West African countries. When fax machines became commonplace, perpetrators quickly reached many more victims with less effort. The Internet and email further revolutionized AFF operations.

Today, these schemes are global, emanating from many other countries.[82] The spamming networks involved often have short lives focusing on specific schemes.[83] Recent estimates suggest that AFF networks may have swindled over $2 billion from U.S. companies and citizens in 2009.[84] In February 2006, three men were arrested in Amsterdam for running an AFF scam that enticed

U.S. victims into believing they were helping charities distribute money. The fraud netted more than $1.2 million. The three pleaded guilty to conspiracy and wire fraud.[85] Estimates indicate that today's AFF networks only need to dupe 1% of the people or businesses they reach to turn a profit.[86]

Cyberspace, Electronic Information, and Organized Crime

As the history of AFF may indicate, organized criminals have adapted to the digital age by becoming expert at stealing information stored and shared electronically. Many are adept at manipulating and defrauding victims in the virtual world. All of this covers a range of activity including cyber intrusions into corporate databases, the theft of individual consumer credit card information, and a wide variety of fraudulent online activity. The criminal groups operating in cyberspace can be broken into two categories: (1) part-timers—those who leverage digital information to enhance other activities, and (2) full-timers—those who solely commit and specialize in online or digital crimes.[87] While this is a helpful distinction to draw for discussion purposes, it is difficult to attribute specific volumes of criminal activity to each category of actors. General statistics suggest that organized criminals from both categories play a large role in online data theft. For instance, in selected data breaches investigated by Verizon and the U.S. Secret Service (USSS) involving businesses around the globe during 2009, 85% of compromised computer records were attributed to organized crime. As 94% of all compromised records in this study were in the financial services sector, many of those records targeted by organized criminals were likely from financial organizations as well.[88]

Online Identity Theft and Sophisticated Credit Card Fraud

Organized criminals are involved in stealing the identities of online consumers and have engaged in technologically advanced credit card fraud. These illicit ventures pilfer from the bank accounts of ordinary citizens and often cast a wide net to maximize the number of victims.

Some organized crime groups have stolen money from victims on intenet auction sites such as eBay. For example, on March 13, 2010, Georgi Boychev Georgiev, a Bulgarian national pleaded guilty in U.S. federal court to laundering money for a transnational criminal network involved in eBay fraud.

The scam did not physically exist in the United States, but it accrued more than $1.4 million from U.S. victims in 2005 and 2006. The network posted fraudulent advertisements on eBay and used a ruse dubbed "eBay Secure Traders" to bilk people out of cash that was wired directly into Eastern European bank accounts.[89] In another case from April 2010, Romanian law enforcement, the FBI, and USSS cooperated in the dismantling an alleged eBay fraud ring that purportedly involved 70 individuals from what have been described in media sources as three different organized cybercrime groups. According to news reports, the scheme included hijacking the eBay accounts of legitimate consumers and then using the hijacked accounts to stage fake sales of non-existent merchandise on eBay. Fraudsters purportedly scammed bidders from Spain, Italy, France, New Zealand, Denmark, Sweden, Germany, Austria, Canada, Switzerland, and the United States, generating $1 million in profits since 2006.[90]

Eurasian criminals in California are engaging in identity theft in which they leverage technological savvy, old-school organized crime strategies, and Internet connectivity to reap thousands of dollars in profits. In 2009 in the city of Redondo Beach in Southern California, Armenian or Russian criminals allegedly targeted a gas station with an Armenian owner (exploiting their own ethnic group). They placed one of their crew members as an employee at the station, where he implanted high-tech skimming devices at gas pumps to steal customer credit card information, victimizing more than 1,000 individuals, including Redondo Beach police officers. The employee quit work and the group made off with more than $300,000 from people's accounts.[91] Another case, this time in the Las Vegas area in 2008, involved an alleged Armenian criminal group that reportedly skimmed more than 1,000 credit and debit cards using insiders at restaurants, bars, and smoke shops. In some instances, the crew manufactured its own cards using stolen information.[92] Losses approached $1.5 million.[93] In 2009, Las Vegas authorities also uncovered a skimming scheme complete with a credit card manufacturing lab.[94] This crew used skimmers that captured information from magnetic strips on credit cards as well as pin numbers using a camera.[95]

In March 2010, Albert Gonzalez, the leader of the largest identity theft and retail hacking ring prosecuted by the United States, was sentenced to 20 years in prison.[96] Through "wardriving"—a technique in which individuals drive around in a car with a laptop computer and search for unsecured wireless networks—the ring hacked into credit card payment systems at retailers including TJX Companies, BJ's Wholesale Club, OfficeMax, Boston Market, Barnes & Noble and Sports Authority, and stole more than 40 million credit and debit card numbers. Gonzalez also provided malware to hackers to aid them in evading anti-virus programs and firewalls in order to access companies' networks and payment systems. The conspirators, located in the United States, Ukraine, and Estonia, laundered their illicit proceeds through banks in Eastern Europe.

Organized Retail Crime and Online Fencing

While not necessarily viewed as "organized crime" by U.S. law enforcement agencies, as its name implies organized retail crime (ORC), or organized retail theft, bears some of the hallmarks of organized criminal activity. ORC typically refers to large-scale retail theft and fraud by organized groups of professional shoplifters, or "boosters."[97] ORC involves a host of retail crimes ranging from retail, manufacturing, distribution, and cargo theft to gift card fraud, receipt fraud, and ticket switching.[98] The organized crime rings resell illegally acquired merchandise in a variety of fencing operations such as flea markets, swap meets, pawn shops, and, more recently, online marketplaces. Most stolen merchandise is sold to a low-level fence, commonly called a "street fence." Street fences will either sell these goods directly to the public or will sell the merchandise to mid-level fences who run "cleaning operations" that remove security tags and store labels as well as repackage stolen goods so they appear as though they came directly from the manufacturer. This "cleaning" may even involve changing the expiration date on perishable goods such as over-the-counter medication and infant formula.

Globalization and technological innovation have allowed more and more transactions to take place online rather than face-to-face. This holds true for retail crime, where thieves have turned to "e-fencing"—using the Internet and online marketplaces as means to fence ill-gotten goods.[99] This has increased criminals' anonymity, global reach, and profitability. Online markets allow criminals to easily distribute stolen goods across the nation and around the globe. E-fencing has also proven to be more profitable to criminals than has fencing at physical locations. While criminals may profit about 30 cents on the dollar (30% of the retail price) by selling goods at physical fencing locations, they can make about 70 cents on the dollar via e-fencing.[100]

A criminal network based in Baltimore serves as an example of an operation that integrated traditional as well as more technologically advanced fencing techniques. As of September 2010, at least 10 defendants, including the owners of pawn shops implicated in the scheme, had pleaded guilty to roles in this organized retail crime ring.[101] In this conspiracy, boosters stole products, including over-the-counter medications, health and beauty aids, gift cards, DVDs, and tools, from retailers such as Target, Safeway, Wal-Mart, and Kohl's. Several pawn shops bought these stolen goods from boosters, cleaned them, and then transported them to other locations for resale. Some co-conspirators used online marketplaces such as eBay and Amazon.com to fence the stolen goods. In all, the case involved about $20 million in stolen goods.

Bulk Narcotics Smuggling and Technology

Technological advances have transformed cocaine and other narcotics trafficking. In the early 1990s, Colombian traffickers—moving narcotics to the United States and elsewhere around the globe—began experimenting with semisubmersible maritime smuggling vessels, which at first were likely too impractical, costly, and risky to operate. Hybrids of traditional submarines and boats, these craft have small above-water profiles—about 18 inches. Increased law enforcement seizures of cocaine shipments carried by more traditional surface vessels encouraged traffickers to adopt semisubmersible technology.[102] Colombian traffickers likely co-opted experts from the legitimate world to develop this technology. Most often, semisubmersibles are used to move product from coastal areas to boats waiting on the open seas. While their current use likely responds in part to interdiction pressures, it also reflects the global availability of expertise, designs, and materials. Vast illicit global cocaine markets have also made such endeavors possible, producing huge profits for traffickers that are then tilled into technology to circumvent law enforcement. But semisubmersibles, which account for 27% of the maritime movement of cocaine toward the United States, themselves are not immune to capture.[103] Since 2006, law enforcement has regularly seized semisubmersible cocaine smuggling vessels from Colombian drug traffickers on the high seas or in clandestine shipyards hidden in coastal mangrove swamps. The Drug Trafficking Vessel Interdiction Act of 2008 (P.L. 110-407) enhanced the federal government's ability to prosecute traffickers operating submersible and semisubmersible vessels by making it a federal crime to operate, embark on, or conspire to operate these vessels in international waters with the intent to avoid detection.

In early July 2010, police in Ecuador seized a fiberglass submarine designed to operate *fully submerged* at a depth of 65 feet. The diesel-powered, twin-screw sub, a marked step forward in technology, was likely intended to transport cocaine on the high seas and could carry 10 tons of cocaine on a 10-day voyage. This vessel represented a large improvement over the semisubmersibles that have been regularly seized from traffickers since 2006.[104]

Mexican drug traffickers have increasingly relied upon ultralight aircraft[105] to smuggle drugs across the Southwest border into the United States. These small planes can fly as low as tree level and are less easily detected than the larger aircrafts that were used by the traffickers prior to 2007.[106] While some traffickers may land the ultralights on the U.S. side of the border to pass off drug loads to distributors, others attach drop baskets that can carry over 300 pounds of marijuana or other drugs. These drop baskets release packages of drugs that will fall to the ground when a lever in the aircraft is activated, and then local gangs or traffickers can pick up and distribute the drugs. In May 2009, a low-flying ultralight aircraft carrying about 275 pounds of marijuana, estimated to be worth $220,480, crashed in Yuma, AZ. The pilot escaped, but two suspected coconspirators were arrested.[107]

Cross-Border Tunnels

Mexican drug traffickers rely on the use of underground, cross-border tunnels to smuggle drugs from Mexico into the United States. Tunneling, while not in and of itself a new tool—having been used for hundreds of years during conflicts and for escapes—has increased not only in prevalence but in sophistication.[108] Early tunnels were rudimentary, "gopher hole" tunnels dug on the Mexican side of the border, traveling just below the surface, and popping out on the U.S. side as close as 100 feet from the border. Slightly more advanced tunnels began to rely on existing infrastructure, which may be shared by neighboring border cities such as the tunnel shared by Nogales, AZ, in the United States and Nogales, Sonora, in Mexico. These interconnecting tunnels may tap into storm drains or sewage systems in order to move drugs even further than smugglers could move them by digging tunnels alone. The most sophisticated tunnels can have rail, ventilation, and electrical systems. The most extensive of such tunnels discovered to date was found in January 2006 in Otay Mesa, CA. This tunnel, stretching nearly three-quarters of a mile in length and traveling over 85 feet below the surface of the earth, resulted in the seizure of more than two tons of marijuana.[109] It had lighting, ventilation, and groundwater drainage systems.

More recently, in November 2010, the San Diego Tunnel Task Force—created in 2003 as a partnership between the U.S. Immigration and Customs Enforcement (ICE), DEA, and the U.S. Border Patrol working along with state law enforcement and Mexican counterparts—uncovered a 600-yard tunnel stretching from Tijuana to Otay Mesa. About 30 tons of marijuana, with an estimated street value of about $20 million, were seized in the United States and Mexico.[110]

U.S. law enforcement uses various tactics and simultaneously faces numerous challenges in detecting these cross-border tunnels. About 125 tunnels have been discovered since the 1990s— primarily in Arizona and California—and more than 75 of these have been found since 2006.[111] One such method of tunnel detection is the use of ground penetrating radar (GPR).[112] However, this technology is limited by factors including soil conditions, tunnel diameter, and tunnel depth. Law enforcement may also use sonic equipment to detect the sounds of digging and tunnel construction and seismic technologies to detect blasts that may be linked to tunnel excavation. U.S. officials have acknowledged that law enforcement currently does not have technology that is reliably able to detect sophisticated tunnels.[113] Rather, tunnels are more effectively discovered as a result of human intelligence and tips rather than technology.

Exploitation of Ethnic Diaspora Communities

Criminal organizations structured along ethnic lines sometimes base their operations in immigrant communities. They use these enclaves to provide cover for their dealings and occasionally also exploit their ethnic compatriots. Historically, criminal groups have burrowed into local ethnic communities, but now this is enhanced by the fact that they can leverage Internet connectivity and extensive, international transportation linkages from localities around the globe. A number of recent cases highlight these issues.

In October 2010, a total of 73 individuals were indicted in the largest single Medicare fraud ever charged.[118] As described by DOJ, the Mirzoyan-Terdjanian organization, an Armenian criminal group, ran fake clinics in 25 states, but had its leadership based in Los Angeles and New York City,[119] two areas with large immigrant populations from the former Soviet Union, (e.g., Glendale, in the Los Angeles region, is home to 200,000 Armenian Americans). According to the president of the Los Angeles chapter of the Armenian-American Chamber of Commerce, this community is exploited by a handful of criminals who were "raised under communist rule in the former Soviet republic of Armenia, where exploiting a corrupt government was seen as fair game."[120]

Organized Crime and Health Care Fraud

Acting Deputy Attorney General Gary G. Grinder recently stated that "the emergence of international organized crime in domestic health care fraud schemes signals a dangerous expansion that poses a serious threat to consumers"[114] The health care system as well as both public and private assistance programs have been targets of individual scammers and organized criminals alike. Criminals steal the identities—or create fake identities— of medical providers, clinics and businesses, and patients. According to the most recent data, in FY2009 U.S. Attorneys opened 1,014 health care fraud investigations, encompassing 1,786 defendants.[115] Aside from the Mirzoyan-Terdjanian organization recently indicted by DOJ, other criminal networks—Eurasian and Nigerian groups—involved in large-scale health care fraud in Los Angeles have recently been caught by U.S. law enforcement. According to news reports, organized crime has turned to targeting Medicare and Medicaid for profit.[116] It is very likely that the groups in Los Angeles favored stealing doctor and patient identities for fraudulent billing over more violent and less lucrative criminal activity. One expert has suggested, "[Health care fraud is] lucrative and it's safe for them [organized criminals]. Why rob a bank and risk getting shot when you can click a mouse and bill Medicare or Medicaid, basically lie on some forms and make millions of dollars doing so."[117]

Members of the Mirzoyan-Terdjanian group allegedly billed Medicare for more than $163 million in fraudulent medical services. They reaped about $35 million in profits. The case involves the stolen identities of both doctors and Medicare beneficiaries and the creation of at least 118 spurious medical clinics across at least 25 states, all part of a largely "virtual" operation. FBI Assistant Director in Charge Janice K. Fedarcyk described the organization as

> completely notional. There were no real medical clinics behind the fraudulent billings, just stolen doctors' identities. There were no colluding patients signing in at the clinics for unneeded treatments, just stolen patient identities. The whole doctor-patient interaction was a mirage. But the money was real, while it lasted.[121]

The indictment in the case also linked Armen Kazarian to the scheme. Arrested in Los Angeles, Kazarian, an Armenian residing in the United States, had substantial influence in the criminal underworld as a *vor v zakone*, a Russian term meaning "thief-in-law."[122] Kazarian had reputedly lied to federal authorities to obtain asylum after emigrating to the United States in 1996.[123] In the course of the scheme, Kazarian mediated disputes for the Mirzoyan-Terdjanian group and allegedly threatened to assault and kill an associate. The indictment suggests that members of the organization, many of them Armenian nationals or immigrants, sent criminal proceeds to Armenia, purchasing real estate and operating businesses with the funds.[124]

In June 2010, DOJ charged five Ukrainian brothers with extortion and conspiring to engage in a pattern of racketeering activity. This far-flung operation based out of Philadelphia and Ukraine had allegedly trafficked about 30 Ukrainians into the United States via Mexico, exploiting them in cleaning crews operating in stores, private residences, and office buildings in Pennsylvania, New York, New Jersey, Maryland, and Washington, DC. According to DOJ, the brothers failed to pay their victims, threatened them with violence, physically abused them, and housed them in overcrowded quarters. One of the brothers is accused of raping a trafficked woman on several occasions.[125] The victims of this scheme likely trusted the brothers as immigrants who had ties to the United States and were willing to help others start new lives in the country.

In another case, at least five Chinese citizens involved in operating Asian massage parlors in Kansas were sentenced between April and October of 2009 for their roles in exploiting Chinese women in the United States.[126] The defendants recruited women from China to work in the United States as masseuses. They then confiscated the women's identification documents and used these documents to fraudulently wire proceeds from illegal activities back to China. They forced the women to work for 14 hours every day, locked them inside the massage parlors to sleep at night, and forced them to perform sexual services for the male patrons of the massage parlors.

West African criminal networks specializing in AFF operate in many nations including the United States, where members have assimilated into local ethnic communities. Many West African fraudsters based outside of their home countries direct proceeds back to organizations in their homelands. More recently, it appears that some of these diaspora-based criminals are operating independently and retaining their ill-gotten gains.[127]

Changing Structures

The traditional image of organized crime involves elaborate hierarchies, behavioral codes, and initiation rituals. Some criminal organizations like the

Cosa Nostra retain a strong element of hierarchy. However, in the last 20 years the criminal underworld has likely moved away from rigid hierarchical organizational structures and toward decentralized and more flexible "network" models. One scholar has argued that the public, and presumably policymakers, are still wedded to hierarchical archetypes particularly when conceptualizing how smugglers operate:

> Still infused with images of cartels and syndicates—rigid, top-down organizations—we are not accustomed to thinking of flexible, even unchartable networks of intermediaries that operate across many borders and provide different services. Some are permanently linked and others vary in their composition, activities, and geographical scope depending on markets and circumstances. Thus, brokers and agents with access to multiple suppliers, conveyors, and buyers are more significant in the drug trade than are old-fashioned "kingpins." For all these brokers, expanding into new product lines, legal or illegal is just a logical business step.[128]

As discussed elsewhere, criminals (much like legitimate businesses) have internationalized their operations, particularly in the last two decades. The fast movement of people, goods, and information stimulated by globalization and technological change has encouraged decentralization and outsourcing. Networks are especially suited for this type of environment.[129] Global businesses and criminal organizations now give critical roles to individuals or groups outside of an organization's core that are often physically separated by thousands of miles. In some cases, such as Colombian drug trafficking organizations, law enforcement successes against criminal hierarchies may have encouraged the adaptation of networks.[130] Criminals conduct more business offshore because of the efficiencies offered by the Internet and advances in the world's transportation and communication infrastructures.[131] In the underground economy, these changes have encouraged the abandonment of exclusivity implied by the elaborate codes of behavior, ethnic bonds, and rigid hierarchy that once typified organized crime.[132]

Networked structures shield organized criminals from law enforcement efforts.[133] Beyond its immediate duties, one element or node in a network can have little understanding of the entire network's criminal activity. It is possible for a network to operate without a single constituent part knowing the entire scheme. In larger networks with clear cut leaders, layers of peripheral nodes likely do not know who directs them. Disruption of peripheral network elements by law enforcement may alert core players to shut down the enterprise.[134]

Network Models

Illicit networks broadly follow two models. "Hub and spoke" networks involve peripheral nodes tied to a leadership core. Core players initiate schemes, settle conflicts, and provide guidance to others. In this model, activity moves from core to peripheral players while the peripheral entities do not interact with one another. "Chain" networks involve the flow of information or movement of criminal goods from node to node in linear fashion without a discernable center of gravity or central command.[135] They often lack obvious individual focal points for policing efforts.

Networks can quickly adapt to changing market conditions or the elimination of nodes by law enforcement by quickly recruiting replacement specialists. Unlike hierarchies such as the Cosa Nostra, networks have few membership requirements, initiation rituals, or loyalty tests. These organizations can also shift allegiances easily, opportunistically drawing in participants for specific tasks.[136]

Blurring of Forms

Some powerful criminal groups that still favor traditional hierarchical structures featuring distinct lines of authority simultaneously exhibit networked characteristics as well, especially a flattening of leadership arrangements and outsourcing of some activities to criminals outside their immediate command and control structures. For example, in the United States hierarchical Mexican drug cartels rely on networks to handle aspects of trafficking. Violent U.S. gangs transport wholesale quantities of narcotics into the United States and procure weapons for some cartels.[137] Prison gangs, for instance, are highly structured, and both national- and regional-level prison gangs have formed alliances with Mexican DTOs. For example, the Barrio Azteca prison gang—operating primarily in southwestern Texas and southeastern New Mexico—has partnered with the Juárez cartel and generates much of its money from smuggling marijuana, heroin, and cocaine across the Southwest border.[138] Similarly, one author of a broad study of criminal organizations in Mexico, Brazil, and Colombia has noted that these groups embody characteristics of what he dubs the "Godfather Model"—rigid hierarchy—and the "Facebook Model"—dynamic network.[139]

Advantage: Networks Challenge Law Enforcement

The shift to networked structures may suggest that criminals are more elusive than ever as the illicit world evolves rapidly, while law enforcement "plays by yesterday's rules and increasingly risks dealing only with the weakest criminals and the easiest problems."[140] According to one study, when combating agile drug cartels, a number of impediments hobble law enforcement officials. Most broadly, the hierarchical authority embodied in bureaucratic structures complicates the decision-making process.[141] Additionally, law enforcement potentially faces

> interagency coordination problems that further complicate, and decelerate, decision making, comprehensive legal and bureaucratic constraints to action, and ambiguous incentive structures that undermine some agents' willingness to share information—and others' commitment to winning the war on drugs.[142]

Yet another challenge for law enforcement investigating more-networked organized criminal groups may arise from constraints in extraterritorial jurisdiction. While some criminal actors in a network may conduct business offshore or overseas and federal law enforcement does have extraterritorial jurisdiction to investigate and prosecute individuals who criminally violate U.S. interests abroad, this jurisdiction does not necessarily cover all crimes committed by organized crime groups.[143] Further, jurisdictional issues can present substantial diplomatic and practical challenges for law enforcement.

Disadvantage: Networks Have Exploitable Weaknesses

Some of the strengths suggested by network structure can also be interpreted as weaknesses. Their inherent compartmentalization potentially impedes efficient information sharing, as key players keep peripheral actors in the dark about important aspects of complex schemes. This suggests that highly networked organizations more effectively engage in simpler criminal conspiracies. Decentralization can undermine the development of strategy and slow down decision making. It may also encourage excessive risk taking by peripheral actors who are not controlled by hierarchical roles rooted in rules enforced by the organization. Decentralization possibly also nurtures challengers who compete with core leaders and foster organizational instability.[144]

Corruption

Some criminal networks co-opt or attract participants from the licit realm to use their specialized skills. These skills are especially valuable in a globalized, high tech era in which technology is critical in overcoming geographical barriers that once slowed international trade. Corrupt individuals maintain their status in above-board business or governmental jobs, providing criminals with clean assets, closely guarded information, specialized access, sensitive information, or resources. Corrupt licit-realm actors also potentially lend criminal enterprises a sense of legitimacy.[145] Because of globalization, it is likely harder to disprove a criminal's claims that he is a legitimate businessman, especially if the proof lies overseas or in multiple jurisdictions. The efforts of organized criminals to draw into their organizations legitimate persons can be described from three broad perspectives: grass-roots, private sector criminal infiltration of businesses; co-optation of powerful business leaders; and public corruption.

"Ground-Level" Exploitation of Private Businesses

Non-executive employees or self-employed individuals can provide criminal organizations with highly specialized capabilities in our highly networked age. The possibilities for co-opted private sector specialists are plentiful. The three examples below suggest this.

- Viktar Krus operated a network that illegally brought foreign workers into the United States. He relied on legitimate facilitators such as Beth Ann Broyles, an Illinois immigration attorney who prepared fraudulent immigration petitions for the organization. Broyles claimed that she initially did not know that she was involved in criminal activity. When she eventually discerned that she was, Broyles rationalized her participation by believing that she was actually somehow assisting immigrants. She was among two dozen co-defendants who worked in Krus's network. Additionally, Krus likely relied on bribing hotel employees to inflate the number of workers they needed to hire. Between 2003 and 2008, he used at least 10 shell companies and evaded millions of dollars in taxes while bringing in 3,800 immigrants, many illegally, to work in the service sector and industrial jobs in the Norfolk, VA, region and elsewhere around the United States. He grossed $34 million, forced people to live 12-15 to an apartment, garnered fees from their wages, and charged legitimate businesses $10 per hour for their labor. Krus received a seven-year prison sentence for conspiracy, tax fraud, visa fraud, and money laundering.[146]

- According to DOJ, the Tran organization, a criminal group that cheated approximately 27 casinos in the United States and Canada out of more than $7 million, bribed card dealers and supervisors at casinos to advance its scheme. In what has been dubbed "the largest cheating ring of all time,"[147] corrupt dealers rigged their shuffles during mini-baccarat and blackjack games. The group also used technologically advanced tools such as hidden transmitters and custom software to predict the order in which cards would reappear during games.[148] The organization began its operations in 2002, and the initial indictment was returned against the group in May 2007.[149]
- DOJ's Organized Crime and Racketeering Section is helping prosecute Victor Kaganov in connection with an illegal money transmitting business he allegedly ran in Oregon. DOJ has not publicly linked Kaganov, who was indicted in March 2010, to any organized crime figures. However, Kaganov purportedly opened multiple shell corporations in Oregon on behalf of Russian clients. He used the shells to shuttle more than $172 million via more than 4,200 wire transactions "in and out of the United States to more than 50 countries," according to DOJ.[150] His supposed criminal activity highlights services that organized criminals could potentially use to launder money.

Big Business and Organized Criminals

In his Annual Threat Assessment for 2010, then-Director of National Intelligence Dennis Blair noted that government, organized crime, intelligence services, and big business figures are growing increasingly close in their interactions. He stated,

> an increasing risk from Russian organized crime is that criminals and criminally linked oligarchs [powerful Eurasian businessmen who rose to power in the immediate post-Soviet period] will enhance the ability of state or state-allied actors to undermine competition in gas, oil, aluminum, and precious metals markets.[151]

However, based on open source information, it is often difficult to determine with any degree of certainty whether oligarchs or other powerful international entrepreneurs with interests in U.S. markets or investors have criminal connections.

Russian billionaire Oleg Deripaska exemplifies this difficulty. According to unnamed U.S. federal officials cited in news reports, Deripaska has struggled to maintain a U.S. visa because of his alleged ties to organized crime.[152] Prior to the global financial crisis, he possessed a $28 billion fortune and was the ninth-wealthiest person in the world.[153] He obtained a U.S. visa in 2005, but it was revoked soon thereafter.[154] According to press reporting, in 2009 the FBI set up two U.S. visits by Deripaska for undisclosed reasons on a limited entry permit from DHS.[155] Claims of criminal connections have publicly dogged him for years. But Deripaska has never been convicted of a crime and has strongly denied all accusations.[156] His difficulty getting a U.S. visa may have kept some U.S. bankers from participation in an initial public offering (IPO) involving his aluminum company, UC Rusal.[157] The IPO occurred in January 2010 on the Hong Kong stock exchange.[158]

Like Deripaska, Stanley Ho, a billionaire casino magnate from Macau, has routinely denied accusations of ties to organized crime. According to media reports, U.S. officials have long suspected Ho had links to Chinese criminal groups known as triads.[159] These suspicions recently resurfaced and involved his daughter, Pansy, and a casino venture in Macau. Pansy and Nevada-based MGM Resorts International (MGM)[160] jointly operate the MGM Macau, which opened in December 2007.[161]

Pansy Ho's co-ownership of MGM Macau emerged as an issue for New Jersey gaming regulators because MGM also possessed a 50% share in Atlantic City's Borgata Hotel Casino and Spa.

According to New Jersey law, MGM had to prove "by clear and convincing evidence, its 'good character, honesty and integrity' on a continuing basis" to maintain its 50% share in the Borgata.[162] In essence, the company and its partners had to be found suitable to operate in New Jersey.

It appears that MGM's direct ties to the Ho family were troubling to New Jersey regulators. In May 2009, the New Jersey Division of Gaming Enforcement (DGE) published a report based on its own investigation of MGM's partnership with Pansy Ho in Macau. The DGE report recommended that both Pansy and Stanley Ho be found "unsuitable persons" by the New Jersey Casino Control Commission.[163] The DGE noted the elder Ho's "continued business ties to persons associated with organized crime" and his daughter's "direct, substantial, and continuing business and financial ties to her father."[164] In March 2010, MGM decided to sell its interest in the Borgata rather than sever ties with Pansy Ho.[165]

Corruption of Public Officials

Organized criminals corrupt public employees, especially individuals who have sensitive jobs. In many cases, criminals seek people who have skills, particular access to information, or job responsibilities that lend themselves to specific schemes. For example, some criminals whose operations depend on personal identification documents seek to inveigle employees with unique access to such information, and smugglers lure people charged with protecting borders into their operations.

In August 2010, Vitaly Fedorchuk was sentenced to 46 months in prison for leading a criminal organization in the Cleveland, OH, area that fraudulently procured Ohio driver's licenses and identification cards for foreign nationals. To do so, Fedorchuk's group relied on Sonya Hilaszek, a corrupt employee at the Deputy Registrar's Office in Parma, OH. She also pleaded guilty in the case and received a prison sentence of 33 months. DOJ accused Hilaszek of producing documents for between 300 and 500 individuals. The criminal group charged foreign nationals—many were from Ukraine or Uzbekistan and in the United States illegally—between $1,500 and $3,000 for the documents. Fedorchuk's group also allegedly cooperated with criminals in Ukraine to fraudulently obtain non-immigrant visas from the U.S. Embassy in Kyiv. They purportedly relied on corrupt Ukrainian nationals employed by the Embassy and charged $12,000 per visa.[166]

Mexican drug traffickers corrupt employees of federal agencies charged with protecting the Southwest border. The number of cases involving corruption at Customs and Border Protection (CBP) reported by the DHS Office of Inspector General have risen from 245 in FY2006 to more than 770 (projected) for FY2010.[167] In FY2009 alone, the DHS Inspector General opened 839 investigations of potential corruption regarding DHS employees. Of the 839 investigations, 576 worked for CBP, 164 for ICE, 64 for U.S. Citizen and Immigration Services (CIS), and 35 for the Transportation Security Administration (TSA).[168] While none of these figures establish exactly how many of these corruption cases are attributable to organized crime, they do suggest a growing challenge for federal law enforcement focused on combating smuggling and trafficking groups along the border. In an attempt to prevent corruption, federal investigation and law enforcement agencies may vet potential employees. For instance, in 2009 available resources allowed CBP to polygraph 10%–15% of applicants applying for border patrol positions, and of those who were polygraphed, about 60% were found *unsuitable* for service.[169]

Two cases highlight the potential for corruption by organized crime along the Southwest border. In May 2010, Martha Garnica, a former CBP technician and officer, pleaded guilty to corruption and drug and alien smuggling charges.[170] She played a significant role in smuggling operations for the

Ciudad Juarez-based La Linea criminal organization.[171] In another case, Jose Raul Montano, Jr. was sentenced to 140 months in prison for bribery, cocaine trafficking, and alien smuggling while assigned as a CBP officer at the Brownsville Gateway Port of Entry (POE) in Brownsville, TX. He allowed Mexican drug traffickers and alien smugglers to illegally transport drugs and people into the United States. At the POE, Montano permitted vehicles containing illicit shipments to pass—without inspection—through the lane he worked. In return, Mexican criminals bribed him. By the time of his arrest in April 2009, he received between $8,000 and $10,000 per vehicle.[172]

ORGANIZED CRIME, A "NATIONAL SECURITY" AND "PUBLIC SECURITY" CONCERN

Clearly, organized crime can be seen as a *public security* concern, largely endangering people, businesses, and property. In fact, in 1995 the National Intelligence Council (NIC) produced a National Intelligence Estimate (NIE) on international organized crime that emphasized just this. However, the U.S. intelligence community's view of international organized crime has shifted critically in the intervening years. In early 2010, the NIC issued a second NIE on the topic. While, according to DOJ officials, most of the salient issues in the 2010 NIE are consistent with those discussed in the 1995 NIE, a key difference emerged. The 2010 NIE argues that international organized crime has evolved into a *national security* concern as well.[173] DOJ officials have described these national security threats in five broad categories: (1) penetrating or influencing state institutions—particularly in those states with weak governance; (2) threatening the global economy by infiltrating financial and commercial markets, driving out legitimate businesses, and using a variety of illegal business practices; (3) engaging in cybercrimes across a range of fraudulent activities impacting individuals, businesses, and global trust systems; (4) partnering with terrorist organizations and insurgent groups such as the Revolutionary Armed Forces of Colombia (FARC), Taliban, and Hezbollah; and (5) expanding the reach of drug trafficking such that DTOs ally with other criminal organizations—regardless of ethnic background—and with local drug distributors.

Alleged Eurasian mob boss Semion Mogilevich embodies both the public and national security dimensions of organized crime. In October 2009, the FBI placed Mogilevich on its Ten Most Wanted Fugitives list.[174] He is wanted for leading a financial scheme that defrauded investors of $150 million between 1993 and 1998. The company that he allegedly controlled at the heart of the operation, YBM Magnex, was based in Newtown, PA, and was incorporated in Canada.[175] Mogilevich was also likely involved in laundering money through YBM Magnex and a network of offshore companies.[176] By purportedly swindling investors, Mogilevich ran an operation that harmed members of the public. More broadly—and involving national security interests—the FBI and DOJ have suggested that the reputed mob boss also has his hands in Eastern European natural gas markets and that he uses his ill-gotten gains to influence "governments and their economies."[177] Russian law enforcement arrested Mogilevich in January 2008 on tax evasion charges but released him in July 2009 on an oath not to flee.[178]

Although analysts have assessed organized crime as being a threat to both public security as well as a national security, the scope of these threats cannot be fully evaluated without a clearer understanding of the scope of organized crime.

Issues

Revisiting the Organized Crime Definition

Currently, there is no statutory definition of organized crime. RICO[179] provisions describe organized crime in terms of an "enterprise" and a "pattern of racketeering activity."[180] The U.S. Code does not, however, provide guidance and information surrounding the nature of criminal organizations and their operational structure. There also appears to be a divergence between the RICO provisions and what federal law enforcement—namely the FBI—considers to be organized crime. For instance, patterns of racketeering activity specified under RICO indicate that criminal organizations may be engaged in a host of crimes including, but not limited to, an act or threat involving murder, kidnapping, gambling, arson, robbery, bribery, extortion, dealing in a controlled substance, and other illegal activities. Although drug trafficking is included in RICO's predicate offenses, law enforcement does not necessarily consider drug trafficking or DTOs to be within the purview of organized crime investigations. One reason for this may be that federal law enforcement tends to segment investigations more on the basis of the criminal violation than on the basis of the criminal actor. While legislating a federal definition of organized crime may not necessarily solve this disconnect with law enforcement, it might lead to changes in the way law enforcement views and investigates organized crime.

A second statutory issue that Congress may consider is that of organized crime in the U.S. Criminal Code. For instance, while there is a Chapter (113B) in Title 18 that deals specifically with terrorism and related crimes, there is no centralized section that speaks specifically to organized crime.[181] Yet organized crime has been described as a leading threat to U.S. security. Though the lack of centralization of organized crime-related statutes may not impact law enforcement's abilities to investigate and prosecute organized crime, it is indicative of the approach by which the federal government views it. And, as mentioned, the harm caused by organized crime may not be clearly estimated without a common understanding of what defines organized crime. Building on this, accurately gauging the public and national security threat posed by organized crime may be complicated without a solid notion of the harm it routinely causes.

Congressional Commission

Beginning in the 1950s, congressional concern about organized crime has resulted not only in legislative efforts to combat it, but in commissions and in various series of hearings aimed at gathering information on the scope of organized crime. One of the first such efforts was the Senate Special Committee to Investigate Organized Crime in Interstate Commerce in 1950 and 1951 led by Senator Kefauver. Another example of such congressional attention is the series of Senate hearings on organized crime in 1958 and 1963 led by Senator McClellan. There was also the 1967 Commission on Crime in the United States led by Attorney General Katzenbach. More recently, and particularly since the terrorist attacks of September 11, 2001, congressional attention has shifted away from traditional crime fighting—including organized crime—toward counterterrorism.

Of the more recent hearings involving organized crime topics, focus has primarily been on threats posed by the DTOs in Mexico. While this is one of the most visible organized crime threats—not only are some of the actors exceedingly violent, but this violence is seen directly along the U.S. Southwest border—it is likely not the sole serious organized crime threat to the United States. As discussed, numerous other organized crime groups, though perhaps not as violent, commit crimes that impact the economic stability, public safety, and domestic security of the United States. As such, one option that Congress may ultimately consider is the convening of a congressional commission to evaluate the scope of organized crime. Such an evaluation might help policymakers determine whether they have provided law enforcement with the appropriate tools to combat today's threats posed by organized crime. It may also result in a clarification of how the federal government defines organized crime and consequently how investigative efforts at the federal level are organized.

Incentives for Investigating Organized Crime

While the effects of certain, high-profile crimes—such as terrorism—are readily seen, the aftermath of organized crime is not always as striking, nor does it produce the same negative visceral reactions. Some argue that this may be one reason for the shift in law enforcement attention and resources more toward counterterrorism-related activities and further away from traditional crime fighting activities since the terrorist attacks of September 11, 2001. However, although the effects of organized crime may not be seen in a consolidated attack resulting in the physical loss of life, the effects are far-reaching. As mentioned, organized crime impacts economic stability, public health and safety, and national security. Consequently, some experts argue that there should be some form of incentive (as well as disincentive) to entice law enforcement to target more monetary and manpower resources toward investigating organized crime.[182]

One such form of incentive that Congress may consider is federal grants to state and local law enforcement for training and technical assistance to investigate and prosecute organized crime. There are several grant programs—such as the Community Oriented Policing Services (COPS) grant program[183] and the Edward Byrne Memorial Justice Assistance Grant (JAG) program[184]—through which state and local law enforcement assistance is available for a variety of purpose areas. However, these purposes do not directly specify as a purpose area the use of funds for combating organized crime. Therefore, policymakers may consider a specific grant program providing not only funding, but technical training and assistance.

Other suggestions that experts have put forward involve the use of negative peer reviews to incentivize law enforcement around the world to focus resources toward combating organized crime.[185] As discussed, various state and federal law enforcement agencies investigate organized crime in the United States. As such, one option Congress may consider could be to direct the formation of a domestic peer review system[186] for law enforcement agencies charged with investigating organized crime. Participation in some form of peer review system could be tied to law enforcement assistance and grant funding eligibility.

Coordination of Domestic Efforts

As mentioned, the federal investigation of organized crime matters has not historically been a centralized effort, and there is no single agency charged with investigating organized crime.[187] As a byproduct, there also has not been a uniform definition of organized crime to guide investigators and prosecutors. Each agency has jurisdiction over an organized crime case based on the criminal violations. For instance, organized crime cases built around drug trafficking offenses are generally investigated by the DEA, whereas those cases built around human trafficking cases are typically investigated by the FBI or ICE. However, many organized crime cases may involve offenses that fall under the jurisdiction of multiple investigative agencies. For example, organized crime groups involved in crimes ranging from counterfeiting and financial institution fraud to identity crimes, computer crimes, and money laundering may be investigated by the U.S. Secret Service (USSS), FBI, ICE, and any number of other federal, state, and local law enforcement agencies. As a result of structuring organized crime investigations around the alleged crimes, it is not always clear which agency will take the lead on a particular case. This can lead to inter-agency conflicts, and if case information is not effectively communicated between agencies, each agency involved may not have a comprehensive view of the case. There are, however, several law enforcement fusion centers, such as the Organized Crime Drug Enforcement Task Force (OCDETF) Fusion Center (OFC), the International Organized Crime Intelligence and Operations Center (IOC-2), and the El Paso Intelligence Center (EPIC), that are charged with consolidating and disseminating intelligence on various organized crime matters. Additionally, different agencies across federal, state, and local levels participate in these centers.

For instance, the OFC assimilates information for the OCDETF Program, which targets major drug trafficking and money laundering organizations. Federal agencies that participate in the OCDETF Program include the DEA; FBI; ICE; Bureau of Alcohol, Tobacco, Firearms, and Explosives (ATF); U.S. Marshals; Internal Revenue Service (IRS); U.S. Coast Guard (USCG); 94 U.S.

Attorneys Offices; and DOJ's Criminal and Tax Divisions. These federal agencies also collaborate with state and local law enforcement.

In May 2009, DOJ announced the creation of the IOC-2—housed at the OFC—which brings together the FBI; ICE; DEA; IRS; ATF; U.S. Secret Service; U.S. Postal Inspection Service (USPIS); U.S. Department of State, Bureau of Diplomatic Security; U.S. Department of Labor, Office of the Inspector General; and DOJ's Criminal Division in partnership with the 94 U.S. Attorneys' Offices and the U.S. Department of the Treasury, Office of Terrorism and Financial Intelligence. Unlike the OFC, the IOC-2 has yet to be funded.[188] It is charged with analyzing and resolving conflicts in information on a host of organized crime cases, not solely those that center on drug trafficking.

EPIC was originally established as an intelligence center to collect and disseminate information relating to drug, alien, and weapon smuggling in support of field enforcement entities throughout the Southwest border region. Following 9/11, counterterrorism also became part of its mission. Though these crimes are not exclusively committed by organized crime groups, they may be, and thus EPIC is involved in combating organized crime. EPIC is jointly operated by the DEA and U.S. Customs and Border Protection (CBP), and other participating agencies include the ICE, USCG, U.S. Secret Service, Department of Defense (DOD), Department of the Interior, FBI, ATF, U.S. Marshals Service, Federal Aviation Administration, National Drug Intelligence Center (NDIC), IRS, National Geospatial-Intelligence Agency, Joint Task Force-North, Joint Interagency Task Force-South, Texas Department of Public Safety, Texas Air National Guard, and El Paso County Sheriff's Office.

In evaluating the most effective means to share organized crime intelligence, Congress may consider several options. One option may include increasing support for intelligence fusion centers such as the OFC, IOC-2, and EPIC. Another option could involve the creation of an interagency organization similar to the National Counterterrorism Center (NCTC), but centered around organized crime. Such an organization would be responsible for "analyzing the [organized crime] threat, sharing that information with ... partners, and integrating all instruments of national power to ensure unity of effort"[189] against organized crime. On the prosecution end, DOJ has already announced a proposed consolidation of the Organized Crime and Racketeering Section (OCRS), the Criminal Division's gang unit, and the National Gang Targeting, Enforcement, and Coordination Center (GangTECC) into a single

Organized Crime and Gang Section.[190] This harmonizes the prosecution of organized crime and gang cases, which DOJ has cited as being similar.

One non-legislative option that Congress may consider regarding the coordination of federal law enforcement efforts to combat organized crime is enforcing its oversight over existing fusion centers. In June 2010, the DOJ Office of the Inspector General (OIG) issued a review of EPIC.[191] The OIG found that EPIC's users value its products, but that EPIC could benefit from improvement in fully developing the National Seizure System and coordinating the High Intensity Drug Trafficking Area (HIDTA) program, consistently coordinating with intelligence organizations across the country, maintaining and analyzing current information from all available sources, and creating objective performance measures by which to evaluate its programs, among other things. Similarly, in November 2009 the OIG reviewed DOJ's anti-gang intelligence and coordination centers.[192] As a result of the review, the OIG determined that the National Gang Intelligence Center had not created a gang information database, as had been directed by Congress.

National Strategy to Combat Organized Crime

One component of federal coordination to combat organized crime may be a national strategy to outline not only what the federal government considers to be the major organized crime threats, but how best to combat them. DOJ officials have indicated that the National Security Council is working to create such a strategy, possibly modeled after the National Security Strategy released on May 27, 2010.[193] The strategy may include recommendations on protecting Americans from organized criminals, protecting financial markets, preventing corruption, increasing public outreach, and partnering with the private sector.[194] There have been reports that this strategy may be rolled out by the end of 2010. Subsequently, Congress may evaluate the legislative options and its oversight role to best assist the federal government in partnering with the private sector, educating the public, and helping law enforcement combat organized crime.

End Notes

[1] These law enforcement agencies include the U.S. Federal Bureau of Investigation (FBI); Drug Enforcement Administration (DEA); Immigration and Customs Enforcement (ICE); the United Kingdom's Serious Organised Crime Agency (SOCA); the Australian Crime Commission and Australian Federal Police; the New Zealand Police; and the Royal

Canadian Mounted Police. See SOCA, "SOCA Working in Partnership Worldwide," http://www.soca.gov.uk/about-soca/working-in-partnership/international-partnerships. Intelligence Committee Futures Working Group, *Crime and Policing Futures*, Strategic Alliance Group, March 2008, p. 2. (Hereafter, Intelligence Committee Futures Working Group, *Futures*.)

[2] This report focuses on U.S. agency and federal statutory definitions of organized crime. For a discussion of scholarly definitions, see CRS Report R40525, *Organized Crime in the United States: Trends and Issues for Congress*, by Kristin M. Finklea.

[3] Department of Justice, *Overview of the Law Enforcement Strategy to Combat International Organized Crime*, April 2008, p. 2, http://www.justice.gov/ag/speeches/2008/ioc-strategy-public-overview.pdf.

[4] Ibid.

[5] FBI, "Organized Crime Glossary," http://www.fbi.gov/hq/cid/orgcrime/glossary.htm.

[6] Department of Justice, Office of the Inspector General, Audit Division, *Follow-up Audit of Federal Bureau of Investigation Personnel Resource Management and Casework,* Audit Report 10-24, April 2010, p. 51, http://www.justice.gov/oig/reports/FBI

[7] The five most powerful Cosa Nostra groups are the historically New York-based Bonanno, Colombo, Gambino, Genovese, and Lucchese crime families. See Selwyn Raab, *Five Families: The Rise, Decline, and Resurgence of America's Most Powerful Mafia Empires*, (New York: Thomas Dunne Books, St. Martin's Press, 2005).

[8] FBI, "How We're Organized to Combat Organized Crime," http://www.fbi.gov/hq/cid/orgcrime/aboutocs.htm.

[9] Statement of William McMahon, Deputy Assistant Director for Field Operations, Bureau of Alcohol, Tobacco, Firearms and Explosives and Anthony P. Placido, Assistant Administrator for Intelligence, Drug Enforcement Administration, before the U.S. Congress, House Committee on Homeland Security, Subcommittee on Border, Maritime, and Global Counterterrorism, *Combating Border Violence: The Role of Interagency Coordination in Investigations*, 111th Cong., 1st sess., July 16, 2009, in reference to the U.S. Department of Justice's National Drug Intelligence Center (NDIC), *2009 National Drug Threat Assessment*, December 2008.

[10] Other federal agencies that participate in the OCDETF Program include the FBI, Immigration and Customs Enforcement (ICE), the Bureau of Alcohol, Tobacco and Firearms (ATF), U.S. Marshals, Internal Revenue Service (IRS), U.S. Coast Guard (USCG), the 94 U.S. Attorneys Offices, DOJ's Criminal and Tax Divisions, and state and local law enforcement agencies. For more information on OCDETF, see http://www.justice.gov/dea/programs/ocdetf.htm.

[11] Remarks by DOJ officials at the NIJ Conference 2010, panel on International Organized Crime: Recent Developments in Policy and Research, June 14, 2010.

[12] Jerry Markon, "Gangs, Organized Crime, Will be Focus of New Justice Department Unit, Crackdown," *Washington Post*, July 12, 2010.

[13] Mexican Embassy to the United States, May 25, 2010, http://portal.sre.gob.mx/usa/index.php?option=news&task= viewarticle&sid=297.

[14] United Nations Office of Drugs and Crime, *UN Convention Against Transnational Organized Crime*, United Nations, New York, 2004. In this definition, a "structured group" is "a group that is not randomly formed for the immediate commission of an offence and that does not need to have formally defined roles for its members, continuity of its membership or a

developed structure." Serious crimes include "conduct constituting an offence punishable by a maximum deprivation of liberty of at least four years or a more serious penalty."

[15] Omnibus Crime Control and Safe Streets Act of 1968, as amended (P.L. 90-351)

[16] 18 U.S.C. § 1961-1968. It was enacted as Title IX of the Organized Crime Control Act of 1970 (P.L. 91- 452).

[17] As defined in 18 U.S.C. § 1961, an "'enterprise' includes any individual, partnership, corporation, association, or other legal entity, and any union or group of individuals associated ... although not [necessarily] a legal entity," and a "'pattern of racketeering activity' requires at least two acts of racketeering activity" to occur within 10 years of one another for a criminal organization to be prosecuted for racketeering. Racketeering is defined as any number of violations, including an act or threat involving murder, kidnapping, gambling, arson, robbery, bribery, extortion, or dealing in a controlled substance. See 18 U.S.C. § 1961 for a comprehensive list of the predicate offenses for racketeering.

[18] Frank E. Hagan, "'Organized Crime' and 'organized crime' Indeterminate Problems of Definition," *Trends in Organized Crime,* vol. 9, no. 4 (Summer 2006), p. 127. See also James O. Finkenauer, "Problems of Definition: What Is Organized Crime?" *Trends in Organized Crime,* vol. 8, no. 3 (Spring 2005), pp. 63-83.

[19] Moisės Naím, *Illicit: How Smugglers, Traffickers, and Copycats are Hijacking the Global Economy* (New York: Anchor Books, 2006) p. 16. (Hereafter: Naím, *Illicit.*)

[20] Intelligence Committee Futures Working Group, *Futures,* p. 5. See also United Nations Office on Drugs and Crime (UNODC), *The Globalization of Crime: A Transnational Organized Crime Threat Assessment,* (Vienna: UNODC, 2010), p. 221.

[21] Jharna Chatterjee, *The Changing Structure of Organized Crime Groups*, Royal Canadian Mounted Police, 2005, pp.

2, 7-8, http://dsp-psd.pwgsc.gc.ca/Collection/PS64-9-2005E.pdf. (Hereafter: Chatterjee, *The Changing Structure*.)

[22] For more on this, see Naím, *Illicit*; Melvyn Levitsky, "Transnational Criminal Networks and International Security," *Syracuse Journal of International Law and Commerce*, vol. 30, no. 2 (Summer 2003), pp. 227-240.

[23] Research and Innovative Technology Administration, Bureau of Transportation Statistics, *America's Container Ports: Freight Hubs That Connect Our Nation to Global Markets*, Department of Transportation, June 2009, pp. 7-8, http://www.bts.gov/publications/americas_container_ports/2009/pdf/entire.pdf.

[24] Naím, *Illicit*, pp. 1-8.

[25] See, for example, Gregory F. Treverton et al., *Film Piracy, Organized Crime, and Terrorism*, RAND Corporation, Santa Monica, CA, 2009, p. 27, http://www.rand.org/pubs/monographs/2009/RAND_MG742.pdf. (Hereafter, Treverton et al., *Film Piracy*.)

[26] U.S. Department of Justice, "Attorney General Eric Holder Speaks at the International Intellectual Property Summit," press release, October 18, 2010, http://www.justice.gov/iso/opa/ag/speeches/2010/ag-speech

[27] Treverton et al., *Film Piracy*.

[28] Treverton et al., *Film Piracy*, p. 3; Deputy Assistant Attorney General Criminal Division U.S. Department of Justice Jason M. Weinstein, *Statement Before the United States House of Representatives Committee on Oversight and Government Reform Subcommittee on Government Management, Organization, and Procurement*, U.S. Department of Justice, Prepared Testimony "Protecting Intellectual Property Rights in a Global Economy: Current Trends and Future Challenges," December 9, 2009, p. 2, http://oversight.house.

gov/images/stories/Hearings/Government_Management/Intellectual_Property_Rights/Draft _DAAG_Weinstein_testimony_OMB_CLEARED_with_new_date.pdf.

[29] U.S. Government Accountability Office (GAO), *Intellectual Property,* p. 5 offers the following definition: "'Pirated copyright goods' refer to any goods that are copies made without the consent of the right holder or person duly authorized by the right holder. 'Counterfeit goods' refer to any goods, including packaging or bearing without authorization, a trademark that is identical to a trademark validly registered for those goods, or that cannot be distinguished in its essential aspects from such a trademark, and that, thereby, infringes the rights of the owner of the trademark in question. According to the U.S. Food and Drug Administration (FDA), 'counterfeit drugs' are defined under U.S. law as those sold under a product name without proper authorization, where the identity of the source drug is knowingly and intentionally mislabeled in a way that suggests that it is the authentic and approved product."

[30] U.S. Government Accountability Office (GAO), *Intellectual Property: Observations on Efforts to Quantify the Economic Effects of Counterfeit and Pirated Goods*, GAO-1-423, April 2010, p. 5, http://www.gao.gov/new.items/d10423.pdf defines intellectual property (IP) as "any innovation, commercial or artistic, or any unique name, symbol, logo, or design used commercially. IP rights protect the economic interests of the creators of these works by giving them property rights over their creations." The report describes copyright as "[a] set of exclusive rights subsisting in original works of authorship fixed in any tangible medium of expression now known or later developed, for a fixed period of time. For example, works may be literary, musical, or artistic." The report defines trademark as "[a]ny sign or any combination of signs capable of distinguishing the source of goods or services is capable of constituting a trademark. Such signs—in particular, words (including personal names), letters, numerals, figurative elements, and combinations of colors, as well as any combination of such signs—are eligible for registration as trademarks." Patents are "[e]xclusive rights granted to inventions for a fixed period of time, whether products or processes, in all fields of technology, provided they are new, not obvious (involve an inventive step), and have utility (are capable of industrial application)."

[31] U.S. Government Accountability Office (GAO), *Intellectual Property*; U.S. Chamber of Commerce, "Protecting Intellectual Property," pp. 9-15, http://www.uschamber.com/IP.htm. IPR infringement may also have some positive effects for consumers who may derive benefit from the lower costs of pirated goods. Industry may also eventually generate more sales as consumers possibly develop interest in purchasing legitimate versions of cheaper counterfeit products they have sampled.

[32] According to U.S. Customs and Border Protection, "domestic value" is the "cost of seized goods, plus the cost of shipping and importing the goods into the U.S. and an amount for profit."

[33] U.S. Customs and Border Protection, "Yearly Comparisons: Seizure Statistics for Intellectual Property Rights (FY 2005-FY2009)," January 2010, http://www.cbp.gov/xp/cgov/trade/priority_trade/ipr/seizure/seizure_stats.xml; U.S. Customs and Border Protection, U.S. Immigration and Customs Enforcement, "Intellectual Property Rights Seizure Statistics: FY 2009," October 2009, p. 2, http://www.cbp.gov/linkhandler/ cgov/trade/priority_trade/ ipr/seizure/ fy09_stats.ctt/fy09_stats.pdf; U.S. Customs and Border Protection, U.S. Immigration and Customs Enforcement, "Intellectual Property Rights Seizure Statistics: FY 2008," January 2009, p. 2, http://www.cbp.gov/linkhandler/cgov/ trade/priority_trade/ipr/ seizure/fy08_final_stat.ctt/fy08_final_stat.pdf.

[34] U.S. Customs and Border Protection, U.S. Immigration and Customs Enforcement, "Intellectual Property Rights Seizure Statistics: FY2009," October 2009, p. 12, http://www.cbp.gov/linkhandler/cgov/tradeseizure/fy09_stats.ctt/fy09_stats.pdf; U.S. Customs and Border Protection, U.S. Immigration and Customs Enforcement, "Intellectual Property Rights Seizure Statistics: FY2008," January 2009, p. 13, http://www.cbp.gov/linkhandler/cgov/trade/priority_trade/ipr/pubs/seizure/fy08_final_stat.ctt/fy08_final_stat.pdf.

[35] Keith Johnson, "U.S. Seizes Big Batches of Fake Goods," *Wall Street Journal*, April 26, 2010.

[36] See "Stolen American Autos Clog the Mexican Market," *New York Times,* February 5, 1922, http://query

[37] Eva Dou, "New-York Based Theft Ring Shipped Hot Cars to Senegal," *Associated Press,* June 30, 2010.

[38] Ibid; Rob Sgobbo, Joe Jackson, and Brendan Brosh, "U.S. to Senegal Car Theft Ring Busted, Attorney General Andrew Cuomo Says," *New York Daily News,* June 30, 2010.

[39] Naím, *Illicit* p. 89; Jackie Turner and Liz Kelly, "Intersections Between Diasporas and Crime Groups in the Constitution of the Human Trafficking Chain," *British Journal of Criminology*, vol. 49, no. 2 (March 2009), p. 184.

[40] Jeffrey S. Passel and D'Vera Cohn, *U.S. Unauthorized Immigration Flows Are Down Sharply Since Mid-Decade*, Pew Hispanic Center, Report, Washington, DC, September 1, 2010, p. i, http://pewhispanic.org/files/reports/126.pdf.

[41] Miriam Jordan, "Illegal Immigration to U.S. Slows Sharply," *Wall Street Journal*, September 1, 2010, http://online.wsj.com/article/SB10001424052748703882304575465742670985642.html?mod=googlenews_wsj.

[42] Also, while some drug trafficking organizations may not be directly involved in human smuggling, they may tax the smugglers who wish to use the established drug trafficking routes. For details on Mexican cartels and human smuggling, see David Luhnow and Jose De Cordoba, "Mexican Military Finds 72 Bodies Near Border," *Wall Street Journal,* August 26, 2010, http://online.wsj.com/article/SB10001424052748703632304575450761550490920.html#articleTabs%3Darticle; Josh Meyer, "Drug Cartels Raise the Stakes on Human Smuggling," *Los Angeles Times,* March 23, 2009, http://articles.latimes.com/2009/mar/23/nation/na-human-smuggling23.

[43] Department of Justice, "Sister Ping Sentenced to 35 Years in Prison for Alien Smuggling, Hostage Taking, Money Laundering, and Ransom Proceeds Conspiracy," press release, March 16, 2006, http://www.justice.gov/usao/nys/ pressreleases/March06/sisterpingsentencingpr.pdf.

[44] Ibid.

[45] Department of Justice, "Hudson County Bar Owner Pleads Guilty to Role in International Human Smuggling Ring," press release, September 12, 2006, http://www.justice.gov/usao/nj/press/files/pdffiles/medr0912rel.pdf.

[46] Department of State, *Trafficking In Persons Report 2006*, June 2006, p. 13, http://www.stateorganization/66086.pdf.

[47] Government Accountability Office (GAO), *Human Trafficking: Better Data, Strategy, and Reporting Needed to Enhance U.S. Antitrafficking Efforts Abroad*, GAO-06-825, July 2006, http://www.gao.gov/new.items/d06825.pdf.

[48] Department of Justice, "Six People Charged in Human Trafficking Conspiracy for Exploiting 400 Thai Farm Workers," press release, September 2, 2010, http://www.justice.gov/ opa/pr/2010/September/10-crt-999.html.

[49] Department of Justice, "Four Defendants Sentenced to Prison in Human Trafficking Ring," press release, April 28, 2010, http://www.justice.gov/usao/gan/press/2010/04-28-10.pdf.

[50] Comments by DOJ officials at the 2010 National Conference on Human Trafficking, May 3–5, Arlington, VA.

[51] Mark Townsend, "How Liverpool Docks Became a Hub of Europe's Deadly Cocaine Trade," *The Guardian*, May 16, 2010.

[52] Michele M. Leonhart, DEA Acting Administrator, "Prepared Remarks: Project Reckoning Press Conference," September 17, 2008, http://www.justice.gov/dea/ speeches/ s091808.html.

[53] National Drug Intelligence Center, *National Drug Threat Assessment*, February 2010, p. 29, http://www.justice.gov/ndic/pubs38/38661/38661p.pdf.

[54] Federal Bureau of Investigation, Newark Division, "Federal Agents Shut Down International Smorgasbord of Crime," press release, March 18, 2009, http://newark.fbi.gov/pressrel/ pressrel09/nk031809.htm.

[55] Federal Bureau of Investigation, "Inside the FBI: Albanian Organized Crime," November 27, 2009, http://www.fbi.gov/inside/archive/inside112709.htm.

[56] Department of Justice, "Ringleader of International Drug Trafficking Ring Pleads Guilty for Role in Drug Smuggling Case," press release, February 24, 2010, http://www.justice.gov/usao/pae/News/Pr/2010/feb/ tran_guilty_plea_release.pdf; Troy Graham, "Woman at Center of Asian Drug-Trafficking Ring Gets Nearly Six Year Term," *Philadelphia Inquirer*, August 25, 2010, http://www.philly.com/ inquirer/local/20100825_ Woman_at_center_of_Asian_drug-trafficking_ring_gets_nearly_six-year_term.html.

[57] Brian Seymour, "Global Money Laundering," *Journal of Applied Security Research*, vol. 3, no. 3-4 (2008), pp. 374-375. (Hereafter, Seymour, "Global Money.")

[58] Dennis C. Blair, Director of National Intelligence, "Annual Threat Assessment of the US Intelligence Community for the Senate Select Committee on Intelligence," Office of the Director of National Intelligence, February 2, 2010, p. 31. (Hereafter, Blair, "Annual Threat Assessment.")

[59] William Booth and Nick Miroff, "Stepped-Up Efforts by U.S., Mexico Fail to Stem Flow of Drug Money South," *Washington Post,* August 25, 2010, http://www.washingtonpost. com/wp-dyn/content/article/2010/08/25/AR2010082506161.html.

[60] For a discussion of estimates, see Douglas Farah, *Money Laundering and Bulk Cash Smuggling: Challenges for the Mrida Initiative,* Woodrow Wilson International Center For Scholars, Mexico Institute and University of San Diego Trans-Border Institute, Working Paper Series on U.S.-Mexico Security Cooperation, Washington, DC, May 2010, p. 6, http://wilsoncenter.org/topics/pubs/Money%20Laundering%20and%20Bulk%20Cash%20S muggling.%20Farah.pdf. (Hereafter, Farah, *Money Laundering*.)

[61] A stored value card looks like a debit or credit card, but stores value directly on the card using magnetic strip technology.

[62] Legislation has been introduced in the 111th Congress (H.R. 5127) that would, among other things, classify stored value cards as monetary instruments in order to require individuals to declare to Customs over $10,000 that they are carrying on a stored value card.

[63] Farah, *Money Laundering*, 23.

[64] Seymour, "Global Money," pp. 375-376.

[65] U.S. Government Accountability Office (GAO), *Company Formations: Minimal Ownership Information Is Collected and Available*, GAO-06-376, April 2006, p. 1, http://www.gao.gov/new.items/d06376.pdf. Hereafter GAO, *Company Formations.*

[66] Jennifer Shasky Calvery, Senior Counsel to the Deputy Attorney General, United States Department of Justice, Statement Before the United States Senate Committee on Homeland Security and Governmental Affairs, Hearing, "Examining State Business Incorporation Practices: A Discussion of the Incorporation Transparency and Law Enforcement Assistance Act," June 18, 2009, pp 1-2, http://www.justice.gov/ola/testimony/111-1/2009-06-18-dagshasky-incorporation.pdf. (Hereafter, Shasky, "Examining State Business.")

[67] GAO, *Company Formations,* p. 1.

[68] GAO, *Company Formations,* p. 13.

[69] Shasky, "Examining State Business," pp. 4-5; Seymour, "Global Money," p. 375.

[70] Jennifer Shasky, Senior Counsel to the Deputy Attorney General, United States Department of Justice, Statement Before the United States Senate Committee on Homeland Security and Governmental Affairs, Hearing, "Business Formation and Financial Crime: Finding a Legislative Solution," November 5, 2009, p. 1, http://hsgac.senate.gov/public/index.cfm?FuseAction=Hearings.Hearing&Hearing_ID=88d1a5fb-7312-4e9e-92b2-8558ccd44f22. Legislation has been introduced in the 111th Congress (S. 569, H.R. 6098) that would establish uniform requirements for states regarding beneficial ownership of public corporations and limited liability companies.

[71] Criminal Intelligence Service Canada (CISC), *2010 Report on Organized Crime,* May 2010, p. 12, http://www.cisc.gc.ca/annual_reports/ annual_report_2010/ document/report_oc_ 2010_e.pdf. (Hereafter, CISC, *2010 Report.*)

[72] For information on unlawful Internet gambling, see CRS Report RS22749, *Unlawful Internet Gambling Enforcement Act (UIGEA) and Its Implementing Regulations*, by Brian T. Yeh and Charles Doyle.

[73] On the advent of Internet gambling, see David G. Schwartz, *Roll the Bones: The History of Gambling,* (New York: Gotham Books, Penguin Group (USA), 2006) pp. 488-494.

[74] George Anastasia, "Officials Charge Man Who Allegedly Ran Mob Gambling Website," *Philadelphia Inquirer,* May 29, 2010, http://www.philly.com/inquirer/local/nj/ 20100529_ Officials_charge_man_who_allegedly_ran_mob_gambling_website.html.

[75] International Mass-Marketing Fraud Working Group (IMMFWG), *Mass-Marketing Fraud: A Threat Assessment*, June 2010, p. 3. (Hereafter, IMMFWG, *Mass Marketing Fraud.*) The IMMFWG includes law enforcement, regulatory, and consumer protection agencies from Australia, Belgium, Canada, the Netherlands, Nigeria, the United Kingdom, and the United States. Europol is also involved.

[76] IMMFWG, *Mass Marketing Fraud*, p. 14.

[77] Ibid.

[78] Chad Bray, "FBI Raids Alleged Boiler Room," *Wall Street Journal,* June 10, 2010, http://online.wsj.com/article/SB10001424052748703890904575297220025441524.html.

[79] Federal Bureau of Investigation, "Common Fraud Schemes," http://www.fbi.gov/majcases/fraud/fraudschemes.htm.

[80] Federal Bureau of Investigation, Detroit Division, "Scam E-Mail/Letter Claiming To Be Associated with FBI Detroit SAC Arena," press release, May 25, 2010, http://detroit.fbi.gov/pressrel/pressrel10/de052510.htm.

[81] Harvey Glickman, "The Nigerian '419' Advance Fee Scams: Prank or Peril?," *Canadian Journal of African Studies*, vol. 39, no. 3 (2005), pp. 463-476.

[82] Edward Fokuoh Ampratwum, "Advance Fee Fraud, '419,' and Investor Confidence in the Economies of Sub-Saharan Africa (SSA) ," *Journal of Financial Crime*, vol. 16, no. 1 (2009), pp. 68-69.

[83] Matthew Zook, "Your Urgent Assistance Is Required: The Intersection of 419 Spam and New Networks of Imagination," *Ethics, Place, and Environment*, vol. 10, no. 1 (March 2007), pp. 66-70.

[84] Jeremy Kirk, "Advance Fee Fraud Scams Rise Dramatically in 2009," *Compuworld*, January 28, 2010, http://www.computerworld.com/s/article/9149890/Advance_fee_fraud

[85] Jeremy Kirk, "Three Spammers Sentenced in U.S. for Advance Fee Fraud," *Network World*, April 3, 2009, http://www.networkworld.com/news/2009/040309-three-spammers-sentenced-in-us.html.

[86] Blaise J. Bergiel, Erich B. Bergiel, and Phillip W. Balsmeir, "Internet Cross Border Crime: A Growing Problem," *Journal of Website Promotion*, vol. 3, no. 3/4 (2008), p. 135.

[87] This parallels the first two elements in Kim-Kwang Raymond Choo's three-part typology of criminal activity in cyberspace. The typology includes "(1) traditional organized crime groups which make use of ICT [information and communications technologies] to enhance their terrestrial criminal activities; (2) organized cybercrime groups which operate exclusively online; and (3) organized groups of ideologically and politically motivated individuals who make use of ICT to facilitate their criminal conduct." See Kim-Kwang Raymond Choo, "Organized Crime Groups in Cyberspace: A Typology," *Trends in Organized Crime,* vol. 11, no. 3 (September 2008), pp. 271.

[88] Wade Baker et al., *2010 Data Breach Investigations Report: A Study Conducted by the Verizon RISK Team in Cooperation with the United States Secret Service*, Verizon, July 2010, pp. 2-15, http://www.verizonbusiness.com/resources/reports/rp_2010-data-breach-report_ en_ xg.pdf.

[89] Department of Justice, "Foreign National Pleads Guilty for Role in International Money Laundering Scheme Involving More than $1.4 Million in Losses to Victims," press release, May 13, 2010, http://www.justice.gov/opa/pr/ 2010/May/10-crm-568.html.

[90] Angela Moscaritolo, "Romanian Police, FBI Break Up 70-Strong eBay Fraud Ring," *SC Magazine,* April 7, 2010, http://www.scmagazineus.com/romanian-police

[91] Paul Teetor, "Russian or Armenian Mob Used 'Model Employee' Con at PCH Arco," *LA Weekly*, June 18, 2009.

[92] Lawrence Mower, "ID Theft Operation Outlined," *Las Vegas Review-Journal*, December 8, 2008.

[93] "Eurasian Organized Crime Task Force Members Arrest 12 Individuals Following Federal Credit Card Fraud and Identity Theft Charges," *States News Service*, December 9, 2008.

[94] "Three Arrested in Credit Card Forgery Ring," KTNV ABC, March 26, 2009, http://www.ktnv.com/Global/ story.asp?S=10065205.

[95] "18 Month Credit Card Fraud Ring Leads to Three Arrests," KTNV ABC, March 25, 2009, http://www.ktnv.com/Global/story.asp?S=10072664.

[96] U.S. Department of Justice, "Leader of Hacking Ring Sentenced for Massive Identity Thefts from Payment Processor and U.S. Retail Networks," press release, March 26, 2010, http://www.justice.gov/opa/pr/2010/March/10-crm329.html.

[97] A "booster" is someone who steals merchandise and then sells it to a fence for a profit. A "fence" is someone who knowingly buys illegally obtained goods from a booster and then sells the goods for a profit. For more information on ORC, see CRS Report R41118, *Organized Retail Crime*, by Kristin M. Finklea.

[98] Ticket switching involves means by which criminals alter the UPC bar codes on merchandise so that the items ring up differently–significantly below the original price–at check-out.

[99] King Rogers, "Organized Retail Theft," in *Retail Crime, Security, and Loss Prevention: An Encyclopedic Reference*, ed. Charles A. Sennewald and John H. Christman (Elseiver Inc., 2008).

[100] National Retail Federation, *2009 Organized Retail Crime Survey*, 2009, p. 8.

[101] Department of Justice, "Pawn Shop Owner Pleads Guilty in Scheme to Launder $20 Million in Proceeds of Stolen Merchandise: Admitted Laundering Millions of Dollars in Proceeds of Stolen Over-the-Counter Medicines, Health and Beauty Aid Products, Gift Cards, DVDs, Tools, and Other Items," press release, September 3, 2010, http://baltimore.fbi.gov/dojpressrel/pressrel10/ba090310a.htm.

[102] Steven S. Dudley, *Drug Trafficking Organizations in Central America: Transportistas, Mexican Cartels, and Maras*, Woodrow Wilson International Center For Scholars, Mexico Institute and University of San Diego Trans-Border Institute, Working Paper Series on U.S.-Mexico Security Cooperation, Washington, DC, May 2010, p. 17, http://wilsoncenter.org/topics/pubs/Drug%20Trafficking%20Organizations%20in%20Central%20America.%20Dudley.pdf.

[103] Rear Admiral Vincent Atkins, U.S. Coast Guard, Testimony before the House Subcommittee on Homeland Security, on Department of Homeland Security Air and Marine Operations and Investments, April 19, 2010, http://www.dhs.gov/ynews/testimony/testimony_1271690315007.shtm.

[104] Drug Enforcement Administration, "DEA Intel Aids in Seizure of Fully-Operational Narco Submarine in Ecuador," press release, July 3, 2010; Chirs Kraul, "Ecuador Police Seize 100-foot Narco-Submarine Being Built Secretly," *Los Angeles Times,* July 6, 2010, http://www.latimes.com/news/nationworld/world/la-fg-ecuador-narco-sub-20100706,0,162212.story; Douglas A. Kash and Eli White, "A New Law Counters the Semisubmersible Smuggling Threat," Federal Bureau of Investigation, March 2010, http://www.fbi.gov/publications/leb/2010/march2010/ smuggling_feature.htm; U.S. Southern Command, "The Self-Propelled Semi-Submersibles Threat," February 20, 2009, http://www.southcom.mil/appssc/factFiles.php?id=83.

[105] The Federal Aviation Administration (FAA) does not classify ultralights as "aircraft." For the FAA definition of an ultralight, see the Code of Federal Regulations (CFR) Title 14, Section 103, http://ecfr.gpoaccess.gov/cgi/t/text/textidx?c=ecfr&sid=77f64066b8e425c 01339f918 e6e9f291&rgn=div5&view=text&node=14:2.0.1.3.16&idno=14. Legislation has been introduced in the 111th Congress (H.R. 5307) that would include ultralights in the definition of an aircraft in order to increase law enforcement's abilities to prosecute drug smuggling cases.

[106] Agence France-Presse, "Mexican Drug Traffickers Using Tiny Planes for US Market," *MSN News*, September 2, 2010, http://news.ph.msn.com/business/article.aspx?cp-documentid=4311772.

[107] U.S. Customs and Border Protection, "Ultralight Plane Crashes in Arizona, Smugglers Apprehended," press release, May 30, 2009, http://www.cbp.gov/xp/cgov/newsroom/news_releases/archives/2009_news_releases/may_2009/ 05302009.xml.

[108] Ken Stier, "Underground Threat: Tunnels Pose Trouble from Mexico to Middle East," *Time*, May 2, 2009.

[109] U.S. Drug Enforcement Administration, "DEA/ICE Uncover 'Massive' Cross-Border Drug Tunnel, Cement lined passage thought to link warehouses in Tijuana and Otay Mesa," press release, January 26, 2006, http://www.justice.gov/dea/pubs/pressrel/pr012606.html.

[110] U.S. Drug Enforcement Administration, "Tunnel Task Force Discovers Cross Border Tunnel, 30 tons of Marijuana Seized in Investigation," press release, November 3, 2010, http://www.justice.gov/dea/pubs/states sd110310.html.

[111] Michael Thurston, "Record drugs haul seized from US-Mexico border tunnel," *AFP*, November 4, 2010, http://www.google CNG.a14f67109bad6c916ff3ce51f338a2d8.3b1.

[112] For more information, see http://www.geophysical.com/militarysecurity.htm.

[113] Ken Stier, "Underground Threat: Tunnels Pose Trouble from Mexico to Middle East," *Time*, May 2, 2009.

[114] Department of Justice, "Seventy-Three Members and Associates of Organized Crime Enterprise, Others Indicted for Health Care Fraud Crimes Involving More Than $163 Million," press release, October 13, 2010, http://www.fbi.gov/ news/pressrel/press-releases/organizedcrime_101310. (Hereafter, DOJ press release, "Seventy-Three Members.")

[115] It is unknown, however, how much of this is attributable to organized crime. For data, see Department of Health and Human Services and Department of Justice, *Health Care Fraud and Abuse Control Program, Annual Report for Fiscal Year 2009*, May 2010, p. 1, http://www.justice.gov/dag/pubdoc/hcfacreport2009.pdf.

[116] Allan Chernoff, Sheila Steffen, "Organized crime's new target: Medicare," CNN, October 24, 2009, http://www.cnn.com/2009/CRIME/10/22/medicare.organized.crime/index.html.

[117] NPR, "Organized Crime Muscles In On Health Care," January 16, 2010, http://www.npr.org/templates/story/ story.php?storyId=122645717.

[118] Department of Justice, "Manhattan U.S. Attorney Charges 44 members and Associates of an Armenian-American Organized Crime Enterprise with $100 Million Medicare Fraud," press release, October 13, 2010, http://newyork.fbi.gov/dojpressrel/pressrel10/nyfo101310.htm. (Hereafter, DOJ press release, "Manhattan U.S. Attorney"; DOJ press release, "Seventy-Three Members.")

[119] DOJ press release, "Seventy-Three Members."

[120] Thomas Watkins, "Armenian Organized Crime Grows More Complex," *Associated Press*, October 16, 2010, http://news.yahoo.com/s/ap/20101016/ap_on_re_us/ us_ armenian_ crime_2.

[121] DOJ press release, "Manhattan U.S. Attorney."

[122] The indictment describes a thief-in-law as "a member of a select group of high-level criminal figures from Russia and the Former Soviet Union who receives tribute from other criminals, offers protection, and uses his recognized position of authority to resolve disputes among criminals, including through threats and instances of violence." See *United States vs. Armen Kazarian, Davit Mirzoyan, Robert Terdjanian, et al.*, Indictment in the U.S. District Court for the Southern District of New York, filed October 13, 2010, http://www.scribd.com/full/39274052?access7m8lpi9tq05hn86c111. (Hereafter, *United States vs. Armen Kazarian.*)

[123] Michael Wilson, William K. Rashbaum, "Real Patients, Real Doctors, Fake Everything Else," *New York Times*, October 13, 2010, http://www.nytimes.com/ 2010/10/14/nyregion/ 14fraud.html?_r=1&scp=1&sq=Real%20Patients,%20Real%20Doctors,%20Fake%20Everything%20Else&st=cse; *United States vs. Armen Kazarian.*

[124] *United States vs. Armen Kazarian.*

[125] Department of Justice, "Five Brothers Charged in Human Trafficking Scheme that Smuggled Young Ukrainian Migrants," press release, June 30, 2010, http://www.justice.gov/opa/ pr/2010/June/10-crt-765.html; Nathan Gorenstein, "5 Brothers Charged with Human Trafficking," *Philadelphia Inquirer,* June 30, 2010, http://www.philly.com/philly/

news/breaking/97508149.html?cmpid=15585797; *United States v. Omelyan Botsvynyuk, et al,* Indictment in the U.S. District Court for the Eastern District of Pennsylvania, n.d. http://www.justice.gov/usao/pae/News/Pr/2010/Jun/ botsvynyuk_indictment.pdf.

[126] Federal Bureau of Investigation, "Leader of Asian Massage Parlor Scheme Sentenced for Coercing Prostitution, Money Laundering, Identity Theft," press release, October 14, 2009, http://kansascity.fbi.gov/dojpressrel/pressrel09/kc101409.htm.

[127] IMMFWG, *Mass Marketing Fraud*, p. 15.

[128] Naím, *Illicit,* pp. 219-220. For a similar discussion that also cites Naím, see Juan Carlos Garzón, *Mafia & Co. The Criminal Networks in Mexico, Brazil, and Colombia,* (Washington, DC: Woodrow Wilson International Center for Scholars, Latin American Program, English translation of 2008 Spanish ed., 2010) pp. 33-34. (Hereafter, Garzón, *Mafia & Co.*)

[129] Phil Williams, "Transnational Criminal Networks," in *Networks and Netwars*, ed. John Arquilla, David Ronfeldt (Santa Monica, CA: National Defenses Research Institute, RAND, 2002), pp. 77-78. (Hereafter: Williams, "Transnational Criminal Networks.")

[130] Scott H. Decker and Margaret Townsend Chapman, *Drug Smugglers on Drug Smuggling: Lessons from the Inside* (Philadelphia: Temple University Press, 2008), pp. 34-36.

[131] Stephen Aguilar-Millan et al., "The Globalization of Crime," *The Futurist*, November/December 2008, p. 42.

[132] Chatterjee, *The Changing Structure*. pp, 2, 7-8.

[133] Carlo Morselli, *Inside Criminal Networks* (New York: Springer, 2009), p. 71.

[134] Williams, "Transnational Criminal Networks," pp. 64-75.

[135] Mette Eilstrup-Sangiovanni and Calvert Jones, "Assessing the Dangers of Illicit Networks: Why al-Qaida May Be Less Threatening Than Many Think," *International Security*, Fall 2008, pp. 12-13.

[136] For networked structures among Colombian drug traffickers, see Michael Kenney, "The Architecture of Drug Trafficking," in *From Pablo to Osama: Trafficking and Terrorist Networks, Government Bureaucracies, and Competitive Adaptation* (University Park, PA: Pennsylvania State University Press, 2007), pp. 25-47. (Hereafter, Kenney, *From Pablo to Osama.*)

[137] National Gang Intelligence Center and National Drug Intelligence Center, *National Gang Threat Assessment, 2009*, January 2009, pp. 11-12, http://www.fbi.gov/ publications /ngta2009.pdf.

[138] Ibid., p. 28. Barrio Azteca members are also involved in other crimes, such as extortion, kidnapping, and alien smuggling. For more information, see Tom Diaz, "Barrio Azteca—Border Boys Linked to Mexican Drug Trafficking Organizations—Part Three," April 17, 2009, http://tomdiaz.wordpress.com/2009/04/17/barrioazteca%E2%80%93border-bad-boys-linked-to-mexican-drug-trafficking. See also the U.S. Department of Justice website at http://www.usdoj.gov/criminal/ gangunit/gangs/prison.html.

[139] Garzón, *Mafia & Co.* pp. 23-24.

[140] Intelligence Committee Futures Working Group, *Futures,* p. 2.

[141] Kenney, *From Pablo to Osama,* p. 132-133.

[142] Ibid.

[143] See the Omnibus Diplomatic Security and Antiterrorism Act of 1968, Title XII of P.L. 99-399. For more detailed information regarding the United States extraterritorial jurisdiction as well as the specific crimes included in this jurisdiction, see CRS Report 94-166, *Extraterritorial Application of American Criminal Law*, by Charles Doyle.

[144] Mette Eilstrup-Sangiovanni and Calvert Jones, "Assessing the Dangers of Illicit Networks: Why al-Qaida May Be Less Threatening Than Many Think," *International Security*, Fall 2008, pp. 16-33.

[145] CISC, *2010 Report*, p. 15, http://www.cisc.gc.ca/annual_reports/ annual_report_2010/ document/report_oc_2010_e.pdf. See also Carlo Morselli and Cynthia Giguere, "Legitimate Strengths in Criminal Networks," *Crime, Law, and Social Change*, 2006, pp. 185-200.

[146] Tim McGlone, "Lawyer Sentenced for Part in Immigration Fraud Ring," *The Virginian-Pilot,* January 26, 2010; McGlone, "Belarus Man Gets 7 Years for Illegal Workers," *The Virginian-Pilot*, July 18, 2009, http://hamptonroads.com/2009/07/belarus-man McGlone, "Prosecutors Tie Illegal Workers to International Crime Syndicate," *The Virginian-Pilot,* January 17, 2009; McGlone, "Illegal-Immigrant Network Supplied Region and Beyond," *The Virginian-Pilot,* January 14, 2009; Bureau of Immigration and Customs Enforcement, "22 Charged with Massive International Visa Scheme," press release, January 13, 2009. For similar examples involving Eurasian organized criminals, see Alexander Sukharenko, "The Use of Corruption by 'Russian' Organized Crime in the United States," *Trends in Organized Crime*, vol. 8, no. 2 (Winter 2004).

[147] Liz Benston, "As Baccarat Grows in Popularity, So Does Cheating," *Las Vegas Sun,* August 30, 2010, http://www.lasvegassun.com/news/2010/aug/30/baccarat-grows-popularity-so-does-cheating/.

[148] Department of Justice, "Former Mohegan Sun Card Dealer Sentenced to Prison for Involvement in Cheating Conspiracy," press release, April 7, 2010, http://newhaven.fbi.gov/dojpressrel/pressrel10/nh040710.htm; Department of Justice, "Leader of Casino-Cheating Criminal Enterprise Sentenced to 70 Months in Prison for Targeting Casinos Across the United States," press release, March 15, 2010, http://www.justice.gov/opa/pr/2010/March/10-crm-265.html.

[149] Department of Justice, "Eight More Individuals Charged in Casino-Cheating Conspiracy," press release, September 18, 2009, http://www.justice.gov/opa/pr/2009/September/09-crm-999.html.

[150] Department of Justice, "Tigard Man Indicted in Connection with Illegal Money Transmitting Business Shell Corporations Created by Defendant to Move Millions of Dollars in and out of United States," press release, March 3, 2010, http://portland.fbi.gov/ dojpressrel/pressrel10/pd030310.htm.

[151] Blair, "Annual Threat Assessment," p. 44.

[152] Gregory L. White and Diana Cimilluca, "Some Bankers Cool on Hot Rusal IPO," *Wall Street Journal*, November 9, 2009, http://online.wsj.com/article/ NA_WSJ_PUB: SB125755269536534861.html. (Hereafter, White and Cimilluca, "Some Bankers.") Evan Perez, Gregory L. White, "FBI Lets Barred Tycoon Visit U.S.," October 30, 2009, http://online.wsj.com/article/ NA_WSJ_PUB:SB125685578903317087.html. (Hereafter, Perez and White, "FBI Lets Barred Tycoon.")

[153] "The World's Billionaires: #9 Oleg Deripaska," *Forbes.com,* March 5, 2008, http://www.forbes.com/lists/2008/10/ billionaires08_Oleg-Deripaska_UCP9.html.

[154] Perez and White, "FBI Lets Barred Tycoon."

[155] White and Cimilluca, "Some Bankers"; Perez and White, "FBI Lets Barred Tycoon."

[156] John Helmer, "Deripaska in 'Russian Mafia' Probe," *BusinessDay,* May 14, 2010, http://www.businessday.co.za/ articles/Content.aspx?id=108965; Misha Glenny, Robert Booth, and Tom Parfitt, "US Refused Oligarch Visa Over Alleged Criminal Associations," *The Guardian*, October 31, 2008, http://www.guardian.

[157] White and Cimilluca, "Some Bankers."

[158] "Aluminum giant RusAl raises $2.24 bln with Hong Kong IPO," *RIA Novosti*, January 22, 2010, http://en.rian.ru/ business/20100122/157651607.html.

[159] Neil Gough, "Triads Thrive in Ho's Casinos, US Report Says," *South China Morning Post*, March 19, 2010. Alexandra Berzon and A.D. Pruitt, "MGM Mirage Knew Ally Was Unfit," *Wall Street Journal,* March 17, 2010, http://online.wsj.com/article/ SB10001424052748704743404575127673757750744.html.

[160] Formerly MGM Mirage.

[161] Tom Mitchell, "Spotlight on MGM Mirage's 'Wild Card," *Financial Times*, March 19, 2010.

[162] State of New Jersey Department of Law and Public Safety, *Special Report of the Division of Gaming Enforcement to the Casino Control Commission on Its Investigation of MGM Mirage's Joint Venture with Pansy Ho in Macau, Special Administrative Region, People's Republic of China,* Redacted, May 18, 2009, p. 1, http://www.state.nj.us/casinos/ home/info/docs/MGM/dge_%20report_redacted.pdf. (Hereafter, DGE, "Report.")

[163] DGE, "Report," pp. 70-71.

[164] DGE, "Report," p. 71.

[165] Wayne Parry, "NJ: Asian Casino Boss Has Mob Ties in China," *Associated Press*, March 17, 2010.

[166] Department of Justice, "Three More Sentenced as Part of Bureau of Motor Vehicle Fraud Ring," press release, August, 19, 2010, http://cleveland.fbi.gov/dojpressrel/ pressrel10/ cl081910a.htm; Patrick O'Donnell, "Parma Clerk Issued Illegal Licenses, FBI Charges," *Cleveland Plain Dealer,* October 30, 2009.

[167] Ceci Connolly, "The Inside Woman," *Washington Post,* September 12, 2010, http://www.washingtonpost.com/wp-dyn/content/article/2010/09/11/AR2010091105087.html. (Hereafter, Connolly, "The Inside Woman.")

[168] See testimony by Thomas M. Frost, Assistant Inspector General for Investigations, U.S. Department of Homeland Security before the U.S. Congress, Senate Committee on Homeland Security and Governmental Affairs, Ad Hoc Subcommittee on State, Local, and Private Sector Preparedness and Integration, *New Border War: Corruption of U.S. Officials by Drug Cartels*, 111th Cong., 1st sess., March 11, 2010.

[169] See testimony by James F. Tomsheck, Assistant Commissioner, Office of Internal Affairs, Customs and Border Protection before the U.S. Congress, Senate Committee on Homeland Security and Governmental Affairs, Ad Hoc Subcommittee on State, Local, and Private Sector Preparedness and Integration, *New Border War: Corruption of U.S. Officials by Drug Cartels*, 111th Cong., 1st sess., March 11, 2010.

[170] Immigration and Customs Enforcement, "Ex-CBP Employee Receives 20 Years in Drug, Alien Smuggling, Corruption Case," press release, August 26, 2010, http://www.ice.gov/pi/nr/1008/100826elpaso.htm.

[171] Connolly, "The Inside Woman."

[172] Department of Justice, "Former CBP Officer Sentenced to Prison for Bribery, Cocaine Trafficking, and Alien Smuggling," press release, March 31, 2010, http://sanantonio.fbi. gov/dojpressrel/pressrel10/sa033110.htm.

[173] Remarks by DOJ officials at the National Institute of Justice Conference 2010, panel on International Organized Crime: Recent Developments in Policy and Research, June 14, 2010. For this report, "public security threat" means threats to people, businesses, or property, and "national security threat" means threats to government, sovereignty, and economic stability. This differentiation is based on John Bailey, *Combating Organized Crime and Drug Trafficking in Mexico: What Are Mexican and U.S. Strategies? Are they*

Working? Woodrow Wilson International Center For Scholars, Mexico Institute and University of San Diego Trans-Border Institute, Working Paper Series on U.S.-Mexico Security Cooperation, Washington, DC, May 2010, p. 3, fn. 2, http://wilsoncenter.org/ topics/pubs/ Combating%20Organized%20Crime.%20Bailey.pdf.

[174] FBI, "Top Ten Fugitives: Global Con Artist and Ruthless Criminal," October 21, 2009, http://www.fbi.gov/page2/ oct09/mogilevich_102109.html. (Hereafter: FBI, "Global Con Artist.")

[175] FBI, "Philadelphia Fugitive Placed on the FBI's 'Ten Most Wanted Fugitives' List," press release, October 21, 2009, http://philadelphia.fbi.gov/pressrel/pressrel09/ph102109a.htm. Jeanne Meserve, "FBI: Mobster More Powerful than Gotti," *CNN*, October 24, 2009, http://articles.cnn.com/2009-10-21/justice/mogilevich.fbi.most.wanted_1_fbiwire-fraud

[176] Williams, "Transnational Criminal Networks," p. 70.

[177] FBI, "Global Con Artist;" Attorney General Michael B. Mukasey, "Attorney General Michael B. Mukasey Delivers Remarks at the CSIS Forum on Combating International Organized Crime," April 23, 2008, *Political/Congressional Transcript Wire*.

[178] "Russian Court Releases Reputed Crime Boss," *The Associated Press,* July 27, 2009.

[179] 18 U.S.C. § 1961-1968. It was enacted as Title IX of the Organized Crime Control Act of 1970 (P.L. 91- 452).

[180] As defined in 18 U.S.C. § 1961, an "'enterprise' includes any individual, partnership, corporation, association, or other legal entity, and any union or group of individuals associated ... although not [necessarily] a legal entity," and a "'pattern of racketeering activity' requires at least two acts of racketeering activity" to occur within 10 years of one another for a criminal organization to be prosecuted for racketeering. Racketeering is defined as any number of violations, including an act or threat involving murder, kidnapping, gambling, arson, robbery, bribery, extortion, or dealing in a controlled substance. See 18 U.S.C. § 1961 for a comprehensive list of the predicate offenses for racketeering.

[181] Some may consider 18 U.S.C. § 1951-1968 (Chapters 95 and 96, Racketeering and RICO, respectively) to be a primary portion of the Code addressing organized crime.

[182] International Peace Institute, *Transnational Organized Crime: Task Forces on Multilateral Security Capacity*, IPI Blue Papers No. 2, 2009, http://www.ipinst.org/media/pdf/ publications/toc_final.pdf. (Hereafter, IPI, *Transnational Organized Crime*.)

[183] For more information on COPS, see CRS Report RL33308, *Community Oriented Policing Services (COPS): Background, Legislation, and Funding*, by Nathan James; as well as CRS Report R40709, *Community Oriented Policing Services (COPS): Current Legislative Issues*, by Nathan James.

[184] For more information on JAG, see CRS Report RS22416, *Edward Byrne Memorial Justice Assistance Grant Program: Legislative and Funding History*, by Nathan James.

[185] IPI, *Transnational Organized Crime*.

[186] Peer review systems are used in a variety of academic, professional, and government settings to evaluate an individual or organization's work or policies. The work or policies are open to examination by other experts and equivalent entities. For instance, the Office of Management and Budget (OMB) has promulgated guidelines for federal regulatory agencies to follow peer review requirements prior to disseminating influential scientific and statistical information. See Office of Management and Budget, "Guidelines for Ensuring and Maximizing the Quality, Objectivity, Utility, and Integrity of Information Disseminated by Federal Agencies; Republication," Vol. 67, No. 36, *Federal Register*, February 22, 2002.

[187] For a discussion of federal law enforcement efforts to combat organized crime, see CRS Report R40525, *Organized Crime in the United States: Trends and Issues for Congress*, by Kristin M. Finklea.

[188] In the FY2011 Budget Request, the Administration requests an additional $15.0 million for the Department of Justice to combat organized crime. $7.6 million of this is requested for funding DOJ staffing of the IOC-2. There were no specific funds requested for the other agencies contributing to the IOC-2.

[189] NCTC mission statement, available at http://www.nctc.gov/about_us/about_nctc.html.

[190] Ryan J. Reilly, "Gang Unit, Organized Crime Section to Merge," *Main Justice*, July 12, 2010.

[191] U.S. Department of Justice, Office of the Inspector General, *Review of the Drug Enforcement Administration's El Paso Intelligence Center*, I-2010-005, June 2010, pp. ii - iii, http://www.justice.gov/oig/reports/DEA/a1005.pdf.

[192] U.S. Department of Justice, Office of the Inspector General, *A Review of the Department's Anti-Gang Intelligence and Coordination Centers*, I-2010-001, November 2009, http://www.justice.gov/oig/reports/FBI

[193] The White House, *National Security Strategy*, May 27, 2010, http://www.whitehouse.gov/sites/default/files/rss_viewer/national_security_strategy.pdf.

[194] Remarks by DOJ officials at the NIJ Conference 2010, panel on International Organized Crime: Recent Developments in Policy and Research, June 14, 2010.

In: Organized Crime
Editor: Jason D. Camilleri
ISBN: 978-1-61324-012-0

Chapter 2

ORGANIZED CRIME IN THE UNITED STATES: TRENDS AND ISSUES FOR CONGRESS*

Kristin M. Finklea

SUMMARY

Organized crime threatens multiple facets of the United States, including the economy and national security. In fact, the Organized Crime Council was reconvened for the first time in 15 years to address this continued threat. Organized crime has taken on an increasingly transnational nature, and with more open borders and the expansion of the Internet, criminals endanger the United States not only from within the borders, but beyond. Threats come from a variety of criminal organizations, including Russian, Asian, Italian, Balkan, Middle Eastern, and African syndicates. Policymakers may question whether the tools they have provided the federal government to combat organized crime are still effective for countering today's evolving risks.

Organized crime could weaken the economy with illegal activities (such as cigarette trafficking and tax evasion scams) that result in a loss of tax revenue for state and federal governments. This is particularly of issue given the current state of the country's economic health. Fraudulent activities in domains such as strategic commodities, credit, insurance, stocks, securities and investments could further weaken the already-troubled financial market.

---

* This is an edited, reformatted and augmented version of a Congressional Research Services publication, dated December 22, 2010.

On the national security front, experts and policymakers have expressed concern over a possible nexus between organized crime and terrorism. Despite the difference in motivation for organized crime (profit) and terrorism (ideology), the linking element for the two is money. Terrorists may potentially obtain funding for their operations from partnering directly with organized crime groups or modeling their profitable criminal acts. Even if organized crime groups and terrorist organizations do not form long-term alliances, the possibility of short-term business alliances may be of concern to policymakers.

In light of these developments, several possible issues for Congress arise. One issue centers on whether the evolving nature of organized crime requires new enforcement tools. Some policymakers have suggested that current laws may not be effective at countering present threats from organized crime. As organized criminals threaten American society from both within and outside U.S. borders, should Congress expand law enforcement's extraterritorial jurisdiction to investigate and prosecute these criminals, and to what extent should Congress encourage multilateral—both domestic and international—crime fighting efforts?

Another possible issue for Congress concerns whether the resources that the federal government allocates to organized crime matters are adequate and appropriately allocated to counter the threats organized crime poses. Following the terrorist attacks of September 11, 2001, national priorities and federal resources shifted away from more traditional crime fighting—including that of organized crime—toward counterterrorism and counterintelligence. For instance, the number of federal agents actually working on organized crime matters and the number of organized crime cases opened in FY2004 decreased relative to levels before September 11, 2001.

INTRODUCTION

Organized crime threatens the economy, national security, and other interests of the United States.[1] Particularly in the past several decades, organized crime has been evolving and taking on an increasingly transnational nature. With more open borders and the expansion of the Internet, organized criminals threaten the United States not only from within the borders, but beyond. Organized crime stretches far beyond the Italian mafia, encompassing Russian, Asian, Balkan, Middle Eastern, and African syndicates. Even though organized crime has not received as much recent media or congressional attention as have other national concerns, such as the threat of terrorism, these criminals have not ceased their illicit activities.

Illustrating that the threats from organized crime remain, former Attorney General Michael Mukasey reconvened the Organized Crime Council (OCC) in April 2008 to address the evolving threats from organized crime.[2] Beyond the individual illegal activities committed by organized crime groups (e.g., gambling, prostitution, labor racketeering, smuggling/trafficking, extortion, theft, murder, and money laundering), the OCC has indicated that these organizations may

- penetrate the energy and other strategic sectors of the economy;
- provide logistical and other support to terrorists, foreign intelligence services, and governments;
- smuggle/traffic people and contraband goods into the United States;
- exploit the United States and international financial systems to move illicit funds;
- use cyberspace to target U.S. victims and infrastructure;
- manipulate securities exchanges and perpetrate sophisticated frauds;
- corrupt or seek to corrupt public officials in the United States and abroad; and
- use violence or the threat of violence as a basis for power.

The domestic impact from the activities of organized crime groups thus extends beyond what many may consider to be traditional organized crime activities. Congress may wish to consider the impact of organized crime on domestic issues of immediate concern, such as the economy and national security. Do these evolving threats from organized crime require new tools to combat it?

Another issue that Congress may wish to consider is the adequacy of the resources the federal government allocates to organized crime. Following the terrorist attacks of September 11, 2001, national priorities and federal resources shifted away from more traditional crime fighting— including that of organized crime—toward counterterrorism and counterintelligence. Subsequently, there has been a decrease in the federal law enforcement resources dedicated to organized crime matters and a decrease in the number of federal organized crime cases opened.[3]

Consequently, the policy question facing Congress is whether the resources that the federal government allocates to organized crime matters are sufficient to counter the threats that organized crime poses.

This report provides a background on organized crime in the United States as well as the tools that Congress has afforded for the federal government to combat it. It outlines the trends in federal efforts to investigate and prosecute organized crime. The report then discusses the evolving nature of organized crime, including the domestic impact of organized crime, prominent organized crime groups, and their illegal activities affecting the United States. It concludes with a discussion of issues that Congress may wish to consider, including the attention the federal government allocates to organized crime matters, the multilateral efforts to combat organized crime, and issues surrounding a potential nexus between organized crime and terrorism.

DEFINITIONS OF ORGANIZED CRIME

A clear definition of organized crime is important for both legal and policy purposes. Some experts suggest that although organized crime is difficult to define, the various attributes of criminal organizations are central to the definition. This report uses the attributes of a criminal organization, in combination with the definitions of organized crime, enterprise, and racketeering as outlined in the current law, as a framework for discussing the trends in organized crime and policy issues for Congress to consider.

Specifically, attributes of organized crime may involve

- structure,
- restricted membership,
- continuity,
- violence or the threat of violence,
- illegal enterprises,
- legitimate business penetration,
- corruption, and
- lack of ideology.[4]

The structure of modern organized crime groups often does not exhibit the rigid hierarchy of more traditional organized crime groups such as the Italian Mafia.[5] Moreover, organized crime groups restrict membership based on a number of factors, including race, ethnicity, kinship, and criminal background. These criminal organizations continue, even if leadership or membership changes over time. Further, violence and/or the threat of violence are integral aspects of organized crime. Organized crime groups profit from illegal enterprises as well as from infiltrating legitimate businesses. They may attempt to corrupt public officials in order to escape investigation, prosecution, or punishment. Notably, the primary goal of organized crime groups is to make money; these groups are profit-driven rather than ideology-driven (a key distinction between organized crime and terrorist groups).[6]

Statutory Definition

There is no current statutory definition of organized crime. The Omnibus Crime Control and Safe Streets Act of 1968, as amended (P.L. 90-351), defined organized crime as "the unlawful activities of the members of a highly organized, disciplined association engaged in supplying illegal goods and services, including but not limited to gambling, prostitution, loan sharking, narcotics, labor racketeering, and other unlawful activities of members of such organizations." This definition described organized crime in terms of the illegal activities rather than in terms of what constitutes a criminal organization. As such, this definition of organized crime could have encompassed the activities of not only organized crime groups, but of terrorist groups and corrupt businesses as well. The definition was repealed in the Justice System Improvement Act of 1979 (P.L. 96-157), leaving the United States with no statutory definition of organized crime.

In the Organized Crime Control Act of 1970 (P.L. 91-452), and more specifically within Title IX—the Racketeer Influenced and Corrupt Organizations Act (RICO)[7]—organized crime is described in terms of an "enterprise" and a "pattern of racketeering activity."[8] The predicate offenses for racketeering include a host of state and federal crimes listed in 18 U.S.C. § 1961. Although RICO provides a definition for an "enterprise," it does not describe the attributes of a criminal enterprise that distinguish it from a legal enterprise. In addition, this definition describes organized crime more in terms of the illegal activities than in terms of the criminal organization.

Background

Organized crime in the United States has a long-standing history. Although this history has its origins prior to the 20th century, organized crime flourished around the time of Prohibition[9] and grabbed the attention of policymakers. Through most of the 20th century, U.S. law enforcement combated what many consider "traditional" organized crime networks operating inside the United States, including the Italian Mafia, Russian Mafia,

Japanese Yakuza, and Chinese Tongs. These criminal organizations were involved in a variety of illegal activities, and in the 1950s and 1960s, the most profitable of these activities was gambling, followed by loan sharking, narcotics trafficking, extortion, prostitution, bootlegging, and fraud.[10] Other prominent activities of organized crime groups were racketeering, theft, murder, and money laundering.

The national focus on organized crime led to several efforts aimed at investigating and controlling it. These initial efforts included the Senate Special Committee to Investigate Organized Crime in Interstate Commerce in 1950 and 1951 led by Senator Kefauver, Senate hearings on organized crime in 1958 and 1963 led by Senator McClellan,[11] a series of conferences on organized crime at Oyster Bay in 1965 and 1966, and the creation of the 1967 Task Force on Organized Crime. This 1967 Task Force reported that law enforcement measures to curb organized crime had not been successful[12] and, further, that organized crime in America was on the rise.[13] Statistics showed that from 1961 to 1966, the number of individuals indicted by the Organized Crime and Racketeering Section (OCRS) of the Department of Justice (DOJ) rose from 121 to 1,198. Further, the number of those indicted individuals actually convicted rose from 73 to 477.[14] Although the raw number of indictments and convictions rose between 1961 and 1966, CRS analysis revealed that the proportion of individuals from organized crime groups who were convicted during this period actually declined, from 60.3% to 39.8%.[15]

Combating organized crime had been a responsibility primarily of state and local law enforcement.[16] As the scope of organized crime was continuing to increase, Congress recognized the need for better crime fighting tools and the need to further the federal government's role in fighting and prosecuting organized crime.[17]

Omnibus Crime Control and Safe Streets Act

One of the first steps taken by Congress to increase the federal government's role in combating organized crime included a series of congressional hearings in 1967 and 1968 and the enactment of the Omnibus Crime Control and Safe Streets Act of 1968 (P.L. 90-351). The Omnibus Crime Control and Safe Streets Act of 1968 was one of the first major pieces of legislation to directly address organized crime. Specifically, it provided grant money via the Law Enforcement Assistance Administration (LEAA)[18] to state law enforcement agencies to combat organized crime. Included in the act was the congressional finding that

> organized criminals make extensive use of wire and oral communications in their criminal activities. The interception of such communications to obtain evidence of the commission of crimes or to prevent their commission is an indispensable aid to law enforcement and the administration of justice.

Title III of this act permitted federal law enforcement agencies to wiretap conversations of suspected criminals, including suspects of organized crime.[19] Electronic wiretapping authority granted in the Omnibus Crime Control and Safe Streets Act of 1968 immediately provided American law enforcement and policymakers with an indication of organized criminals' activity, specifically their involvement in illegally importing and distributing narcotics.[20] Despite these tools to combat criminals, the federal government still lacked the tools to combat criminal *organizations*.[21]

The Organized Crime Control Act and RICO

The Organized Crime Control Act of 1970 (P.L. 91-452) strengthened the ability of the federal government to combat and prosecute criminal organizations. It provided for Special Grand Juries to investigate multi-jurisdictional organized crime; these grand juries are able to produce reports outlining public corruption and organized crime conditions in their respective districts. The act also allowed for witnesses of organized crime to be granted immunity from prosecution in exchange for testimony. Further, it authorized security for government witnesses or potential witnesses in organized crime cases. This measure laid the groundwork for the Witness Security Program (WITSEC).[22] The WITSEC program allows for the protection and relocation of witnesses and their families, whose lives may be in danger as a result of their testimony in organized and other major crime cases.

Title IX of the Organized Crime Control Act of 1970 created the Racketeer Influenced and Corrupt Organizations Act (RICO).[23] Many view RICO as the single most important piece of organized crime legislation enacted.[24] RICO allows for the prosecution of anyone who participates or conspires to participate in a criminal enterprise/organization through two acts of "racketeering activity" within a 10-year period of time. The predicate offenses for racketeering include various state and federal crimes listed in the U.S. Code.[25] Since its enactment, RICO has been one of the dominant tools used in organized crime prosecutions.

Asset Forfeiture and Money Laundering Statutes

Since the passage of RICO, Congress has enacted legislation regarding asset forfeiture and money laundering, both of which have increased the federal government's ability to combat organized crime.[26] The asset forfeiture and money laundering statutes have provided a means for the federal government to further attack the financial structure and assets of organized crime groups.[27] Although RICO included provisions for asset forfeiture, the Comprehensive Crime Control Act of 1984 (P.L. 98-473) expanded upon these provisions. Specifically, Title II of Chapter III—the Comprehensive Forfeiture Act of 1984—amended RICO by specifying that proceeds (both tangible and intangible) obtained directly or indirectly from racketeering activity were subject to forfeiture. This act also established the Department of Justice's Asset Forfeiture Fund in the Department of the Treasury. The rules for civil forfeiture proceedings were later revised in the Civil Asset Forfeiture Reform Act of 2000 (P.L. 106-185), improving the federal government's ability to prosecute organized crime cases. Money laundering, the primary method of concealing the illicit proceeds from organized crime activities or placing them back into further illegal activity, was established as a federal criminal offense in the Money Laundering Control Act of 1986 (P.L. 99-570).[28] This act also established criminal and civil penalties for money laundering, as well as procedures for forfeiting the illicit funds. It appears that these laws have all provided effective tools, as the Department of Justice and Federal Bureau of Investigation have indicated that the three most prominent tools relied upon when investigating and prosecuting organized crime are RICO, money laundering, and asset forfeiture statutes.

More Recent Federal Attention to Organized Crime[29]

Following the terrorist attacks of September 11, 2001, congressional and national law enforcement priorities shifted away from traditional crime fighting toward counterterrorism. More recently, however, there appears to be an increase in national attention to the need for fighting more traditional crime, including organized crime.[30] In fact, after a 15-year hiatus, the Organized Crime Council met in April 2008 for the first time since 1993.[31] The renewed attention to traditional crime fighting—and specifically for purposes of this discussion, organized crime— has increasingly shifted toward the transnational nature of organized crime. Though organized crime has arguably always been transnational, it was not until the 1990s, following the Cold War and the spread of globalization, that the transnational nature of organized crime surged and criminals expanded their operations across increasingly open borders.

FEDERAL LAW ENFORCEMENT EFFORTS TO COMBAT ORGANIZED CRIME

In general, domestic crime control tends to fall on the shoulders of state and local law enforcement agencies. As mentioned above, however, the federal government began to play a larger role in combating organized crime following the enactment of the Omnibus Crime Control and Safe Streets Act of 1968, and even more after RICO and the Organized Crime Control Act of 1970. Various federal agencies are currently involved in controlling the activities of organized crime groups. In addition to domestic efforts to combat organized crime, the federal government is also involved in international efforts.

Domestic Efforts

Combating organized crime is not a task handled by one federal agency or even one department. Many agencies have a hand in tackling the threats posed by organized crime. The Department of Justice, specifically the U.S. Attorney General's Organized Crime Council, is responsible for creating domestic organized crime policy.[32] The council is chaired by the Deputy Attorney General and has representatives from the Federal Bureau of Investigation (FBI); the U.S. Drug Enforcement Agency (DEA); the Bureau of Alcohol, Tobacco, Firearms and Explosives (ATF); the U.S. Immigration and Customs Enforcement (ICE); the U.S. Secret Service; the Internal Revenue Service (IRS); the U.S. Postal Inspection Service; Diplomatic Security; and the U.S. Department of Labor, Office of the Inspector General.

Although many federal and state departments and agencies are engaged in fighting organized crime, the primary agency involved in combating organized crime is the FBI.[33] The Transnational Criminal Enterprise Section in the Criminal Enterprise Branch of the Criminal Investigative Division is responsible for investigating organized crime. This Organized Crime Section is divided into three principal units investigating (1) La Cosa Nostra, Italian organized crime, and racketeering; (2) Eurasian/Middle Eastern organized crime; and (3) Asian and African criminal enterprises.[34]

As a key analytical tool, the FBI uses the Enterprise Theory of Investigation (ETI) to investigate organized crime. ETI involves two steps: (1) identifying a criminal organization and the criminal activities of this organization and (2) identifying the financial assets of the criminal organization for possible forfeiture.[35] This investigative technique seems to complement the RICO statutes in that both ETI and RICO are aimed at dismantling criminal organizations. Further, ETI identifies financial assets that may be subject to forfeiture under civil RICO statutes. This aspect of ETI is directed at combating money laundering and thus the financial lifeline of organized crime.

Domestic Working Groups and Task Forces[36]

Many of the FBI field offices have organized crime task forces. In those regions, the FBI works with state and local partners as well as with other federal agencies to combat organized crime. These task forces may be broader task forces covering a range of criminal syndicates, or they may be more specific covering a particular organized crime group. One example of a broad organized crime task force exists at the Minneapolis field division of the FBI; this division leads an Organized Crime Task Force that combines the efforts of other federal agencies as well as local law enforcement to target a number of criminal organizations involved in various crimes.[37] On the other hand, examples of more specific organized crime task forces exist at the FBI's New York division; in New York, there have been designated La Cosa Nostra (LCN) task forces, some dedicated to specific LCN families.[38] Even if standing task forces are not formed, domestic agencies work jointly and rely on the resources of one another to combat organized crime. For example, when investigating labor racketeering, the FBI may work with the Department of Labor, the Department of Transportation, and the Internal Revenue Service, as well as state and local authorities.

With respect to prosecuting organized crime cases, the Department of Justice Organized Crime and Racketeering Section has Strike Force Units dedicated to organized crime. These units currently exist in U.S. Attorneys' Offices in 21 of the 93 federal districts with a large organized crime presence. The Strike Force Units operate in these particular 21 offices for historical reasons; those are the 21 offices where the LCN has had the largest presence, and the Strike Force Units continue to operate out of those offices. These units comprise a group of prosecutors with particular expertise in large, multi-defendant RICO cases.[39] Ultimately, the U.S. Attorney General is the chief law enforcement officer responsible for criminal investigations and prosecutions, including those of organized crime.

International Efforts

The United Nations Convention Against Transnational Organized Crime[40] is the main international tool for combating organized crime. In 2005, the United States ratified the Convention as well as the companion Protocols on trafficking in persons and smuggling of migrants. Among other provisions, the Convention provides for greater law enforcement cooperation and mutual legal assistance across nations where there were no previous agreements for such assistance. With the evolving transnational nature of organized crime, this coordination with international organizations is essential. Further, with increasingly open borders and the expansion of the Internet, organized criminals threaten American society not only from within the borders, but beyond.

One outcome of increasing transnational crime is that domestic federal law enforcement agencies work with international organizations to combat organized crime threats to the United States. As one example of this cooperation, the U.S. government and federal agencies support the United Nations (UN) Office of Drugs and Crime (UNODC) efforts to combat international organized crime. UNODC helps UN member countries implement provisions of the Convention Against Transnational Organized Crime to counter organized crime problems. Within the Department of Justice, the U.S. National Central Bureau (USNCB) of the International Criminal Police Organization (INTERPOL)[41] is the point of contact for INTERPOL matters in the United States. The USNCB can access INTERPOL's databases, and it coordinates requests for international investigations between U.S. law enforcement and their international partners.[42] Specifically, the USNCB Terrorism and Violent Crimes Division coordinates requests on organized crime cases. Also, the FBI participates in several international working groups and task forces to formulate best practices in combating organized crime.

International Working Groups and Task Forces

Federal law enforcement agencies in the United States and in Italy participate in the Italian American Working Group, which first met in 1984. This working group addresses problems common to both countries, including organized crime, drug trafficking, money laundering, cyber crime, and extradition issues. The Pantheon Project furthers the law enforcement relationship between the United States and Italy. The project provides for two FBI agents that work at the Italian National Police headquarters and for two Italian officers that work at the FBI.

With respect to Russian organized crime, the FBI is involved in international *working groups*, including the Eurasian Organized Crime Working Group, the Central European Working Group, and the Southern European Cooperative Initiative. In addition, the FBI set up a joint FBI/Hungarian National Police task force in Budapest, Hungary, to combat Russian organized crime.[43] This task force was established in 2000 to counter the increasing threat of Russian organized crime and is the only international *task force* in which the FBI is currently involved. The FBI has requested additional funding for this task force in its 2011-2015 budget. The FBI, in conjunction with other law enforcement agencies around the world, has also provided INTERPOL with information on individuals involved in Eurasian organized crime; this information is the basis for *Project Millennium*, a multinational effort, led by INTERPOL, to combat Eurasian organized crime.

FEDERAL INVESTIGATIONS AND PROSECUTIONS OF ORGANIZED CRIME

According to the Department of Justice and the FBI, the threats posed by organized crime have become more broad and complex than ever before. Federal resources dedicated to organized crime matters, however, do not appear to have expanded along with the threats, and have actually decreased since 2001. After the September 11, 2001, terrorist attacks, national priorities, including those of federal law enforcement, shifted further toward counterterrorism-related activities and further away from traditional crime fighting activities. Within the law enforcement domain, this shift can be objectively seen in the field agents assigned to organized crime casework, the cases investigated, and the cases handled by the U.S. Attorneys' Offices.

Agent Utilization

Following the September 11, 2001, terrorist attacks, the FBI reorganized, prioritizing counterterrorism and counterintelligence over traditional crime matters. The FBI did not, however, significantly change its field agent allocation for organized crime matters between FY2001 and FY2004. Agent allocation remained nearly constant at 700, 697, 698, and 720 agents, respectively, for FY2001-FY2004.[44] On the other hand, the FBI *utilization* of field agents in organized crime matters during this time period did not mirror that of the agent *allocation*. **Figure 1** illustrates that the allocation of agents remained relatively constant, while the actual utilization decreased. The Department of Justice, Office of the Inspector General (OIG), found that in FY2004 the FBI utilized 35% fewer agents on organized crime matters than it did in FY2000.[45] While the FBI utilized 682 agents on organized crime matters in FY2000, this number dropped to 446 in FY2004. The questions remain, however, whether field agents continue to be *allocated* to organized crime matters at similar rates to those before the terrorist attacks of September 11, 2001, and subsequent FBI reorganization, and whether these agents continue to be *utilized* at lower rates than which they are allocated.[46]

This disparity between FBI field agent allocation and field agent utilization may suggest several things. For one, it may suggest that organized crime posed less of a threat to the United States in 2004 than it did in 2000. However, recent actions and testimony by former Attorney General Michael Mukasey suggest the opposite may be true. Former Attorney General Mukasey reconvened the Organized Crime Council in April 2008, for the first time in 15 years.[47] He stated that he did so because organized crime—both domestic and international—remains a significant threat. The sustained threat does not explain the decrease in field agent utilization in these matters. A second possible reason for the disparity in field agent allocation and utilization is that although the FBI did not intend to decrease its agent utilization on organized crime matters, agents may have been diverted to higher-priority issues such as counterterrorism. In fact, the Department of Justice, OIG, reported that the FBI confirmed underutilizing organized crime resources because the field divisions committed to prioritizing counterterrorism first and foremost. "Combat[ing] transnational and national criminal organizations and enterprises" is the FBI's sixth-highest priority matter.[48] The FBI diverted agents from traditional crime squads—such as organized crime—and moved them to counterterrorism squads.[49] A third potential explanation is that the FBI lacks the man power and monetary resources to address all significant threats that the country faces. This lack of resources may act in conjunction with the FBI's prioritization of counterterrorism. FBI Director Robert Muller has stated that indeed resources have shifted away from traditional crime fighting, and that there is a need to restore the criminal programs to "appropriate resource levels."[50]

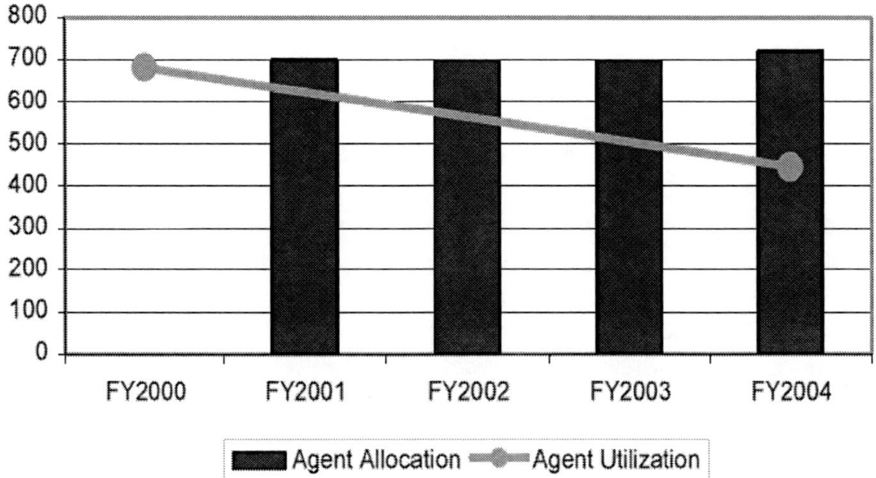

Source: U.S. Department of Justice, Office of the Inspector General, Audit Division, *The External Effects of the Federal Bureau of Investigation's Reprioritization Efforts*, Audit Report 05-37, September 2005, pp. 73-75, http://www.usdoj.gov/oig/reports/FBI

Notes: The data on organized crime agent allocation come from the OIG analysis of FBI Resource Management and Allocation (RMA) Office data. The data on organized crime agent utilization come from the OIG analysis of FBI Time Utilization Recordkeeping (TURK) data. The FBI utilized 35% fewer agents on organized crime matters in FY2004 than it did in FY2000. FBI organized crime agent allocation data were not available to the OIG for FY2000 because prior to FY2001, the FBI allocated organized crime and drug resources together.

Figure 1. FBI Allocation and Utilization of Agents on Organized Crime Matters, FY2000-FY2004.

A follow-up report by the OIG indicates that the FBI's agent utilization on organized crime matters may have continued to decrease between FY2005 and FY2009.[51] In FY2005, the FBI utilized 525 agents for organized crime matters. This declined by more than 15% to 443 agents in FY2009. Of note, the agent utilization data for organized crime matters between FY2005 and FY2009 cannot be directly compared to the utilization data for these matters between FY2000 and FY2004 because the classifications of what constitutes organized crime for these periods differ. For instance, data for the period from FY2005 through FY2009 include agent utilization data for transnational organized crime matters, whereas these are not specifically included in the data from FY2000-FY2004. Further, while the organized crime agent utilization data for FY2000-FY2004 were available, the number of agents allocated specifically to organized crime matters for FY2005-FY2009 is unknown because allocation data were only available for overall criminal enterprise casework, encompassing gangs, criminal enterprises (including Organized Crime Drug Enforcement Task Force cases), and organized crime.

Case Openings

In FY2000, the FBI had 682 field agents investigating organized crime, and they initiated (opened) 433 organized crime investigations (cases) in that year, as shown in **Table 1**. Thus, the number of cases per agent was about 0.6. In FY2004, the FBI had 433 field agents investigating organized crime, and they initiated 263 organized crime investigations. Therefore, the number of cases per agent was also about 0.6.[52] Taken alone, a decrease in the number of organized crime cases could suggest that the threat from organized crime is actually decreasing. However, the number of agents investigating organized crime decreased proportionally to the number of organized crime cases opened. Therefore, using data from the number of organized crime case openings does not alone provide a reliable indication of the organized crime threat. There are several possible explanations for the simultaneous decrease in agents investigating organized crime matters and the number of organized crime case openings. One possibility is that a reduction in organized crime activity—and thus a reduction in the number of organized crime cases opened—could lead to fewer agents needed to investigate organized crime matters. On the other hand, a reduction in agents working on organized crime cases could lead to a reduction in the overall number of these cases opened and may not actually reflect a decrease in organized crime activity. One possible side effect of a decrease in the number of federal agents investigating organized crime may be an increased workload for each agent working on these cases; if the organized crime threat is sustained—as has been suggested by DOJ officials—it is possible that the caseloads of organized crime agents could increase if the number of agents actually investigating organized crime is sustained or further decreased.[53]

Table 1. FBI Organized Crime Cases Worked Per Agent, FY2000 and FY2004

Fiscal Year	Organized Crime Agent Utilization	Number of Organized Crime Cases Opened	Organized Crime Cases/Agent
2000	682	433	0.63
2004	446	263	0.59

Source: U.S. Department of Justice, Office of the Inspector General, Audit Division, *The External Effects of the Federal Bureau of Investigation's Reprioritization Efforts*, Audit Report 05-37, September 2005, pp. 73-75, http://www.usdoj.gov/ oig/reports/FBI

Notes: Data on organized crime agent utilization and case openings include data across the FBI's three organized crime subprograms: (1) La Cosa Nostra and Italian, (2) Asian, and (3) Russian and Eurasian. The data on organized crime agent utilization come from the OIG analysis of FBI Time Utilization Recordkeeping (TURK) data. The data on organized crime case openings come from the OIG analysis of FBI Automated Case Support (ACS) data. There was about a 35% decrease in the number of FBI agents utilized on organized crime matters and about a 39% decrease in the number of organized crime cases opened between FY2000 and FY2004.

Prosecutions

The Department of Justice, Organized Crime and Racketeering Section (OCRS), oversees federal organized crime prosecutions. As noted earlier, OCRS has organized crime Strike Force Units in 21 of the 94 U.S. Attorneys' Offices (USAOs) where there exists a large organized crime presence in that district. **Figure 2** graphs the number of organized crime cases referred to the USAOs for prosecution from FY1999 through FY2010. As evidenced in the figure, there has not been a consistent increase or decrease in the number of organized crime cases filed with the USAOs across these years.

Many factors could influence the number of organized crime cases referred to the USAOs for prosecution. While this number could reflect the actual activities of organized crime groups, several factors suggest that the trends in prosecutions may not mirror the trends in organized criminal activity—either in type or in number. Firstly, prosecutions may be driven in part by Administration priorities, which may not emphasize all federal crimes equally. Secondly, organized crime cases that are actually prosecuted are only a small subset (and not necessarily a proportionate subset) of those crimes committed.[54] Therefore, the number of organized crime prosecutions alone provides little evidence as to the true trends in organized criminal activity.

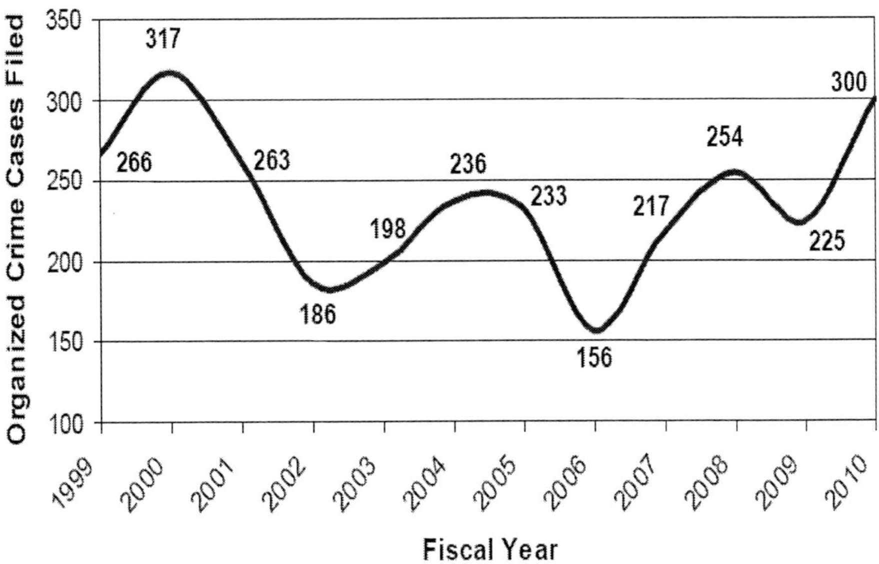

Source: Data provided to CRS by the USAO.

Notes: These data include organized crime cases filed with the USAOs from all federal agencies.

Figure 2. Organized Crime Cases Filed with the U.S. Attorneys' Offices, FY1999-FY2010.

One question that remains is whether the resources and tools for investigating and prosecuting organized crime in the United States—as previously provided by Congress—are the most effective tools for combating today's threats from organized crime.

CURRENT ORGANIZED CRIME TRENDS

As mentioned, organized crime in the United States has taken on an increasingly transnational nature. This shift has been facilitated by factors such as economic globalization and improved communications technology.[55] Organized crime activities across the globe do not appear to be waning, and the National Intelligence Council has estimated that by 2025, the "relative power" of criminal networks will continue to rise, and some countries could even be taken over and run by these networks.[56] The section below provides a detailed discussion of the organized crime groups that operate in the United States, the activities of these groups, and the domestic industries that have been and may continue to be threatened by organized crime.

One way of analyzing the organized crime threat is by examining the most prominent organized crime groups operating in the United States. The FBI, for instance, provides information on the various organized crime groups in order to present a picture of organized crime in the United States. A second method is by examining those areas of society threatened most by the activities of organized crime (such as the economy or national security), regardless of which group is committing the crime. The Organized Crime and Racketeering Section (OCRS) at DOJ, for example, presents the organized crime threats to the United States in terms of the principal threat areas, rather than the individual groups committing crimes. Subsequent discussion uses both approaches to analyze organized crime.

Organized Crime Groups Operating in the United States[57]

Although organized crime is popularly associated with the Italian Mafia, the breadth of organized crime in the United States includes many other criminal organizations. The FBI investigates organized crime groups that fall into three major categories: (1) La Cosa Nostra, Italian organized crime, and racketeering; (2) Eurasian/Middle Eastern organized crime; and (3) Asian and African criminal enterprises.[58] **Figure 3** outlines the top organized crime threats to the United States, as identified by the FBI. Threats to the United States posed by selected large-scale criminal organizations are discussed below.

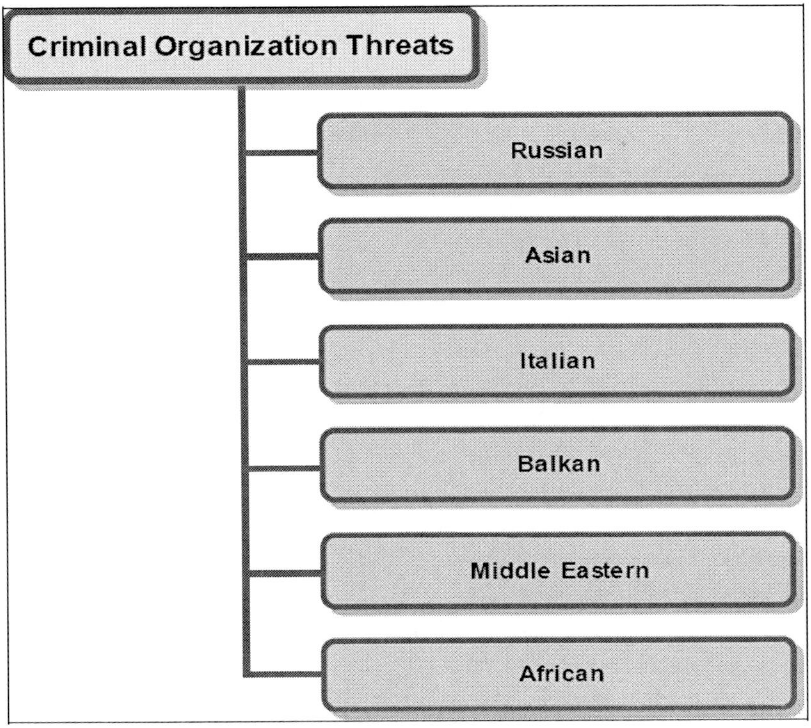

Source: The FBI identifies and provides an overview of these various organized crime groups on its website at http://www.fbi.gov/hq/cid/orgcrime/ocshome.htm.

Figure 3. Organized Crime Threats in the United States According to the FBI.

Eurasian/Russian

The discussion of Russian organized crime tends to reference not only Russian crime syndicates, but a variety of Eurasian crime groups as well.[59] These groups began emerging in the United States in the late 1970s and became even more prevalent following the collapse of the Soviet Union in 1991. They are now considered by the FBI to be the top organized crime threat to the United States.[60] The Russian organized crime groups that operate in the United States exhibit less of a traditional hierarchical structure than the Italian Cosa Nostra, and they form their networks based more on the skills needed for particular crimes.[61] In the United States, Russian organized criminals are involved in long-established organized crime activities such as extortion, abduction, human smuggling, prostitution, drug trafficking, and theft, as well as white-collar criminal activities including money laundering and fraud of various types. In fact, the FBI has indicated that roughly 60% of FBI cases targeting Russian organized crime involve fraud.[62] The types of fraud and scams that Russian criminals participate in cross industries from health care and strategic commodities (e.g., precious metals) fraud to credit card, insurance, securities, and investment fraud. They are also involved in scams in domains such as tax evasion and energy price rigging. Many Russian organized crime groups operate in New York, New Jersey, Boston, Philadelphia, Chicago, Los Angeles, San Francisco, and Miami, among other cities.[63]

U.S. law enforcement has relied heavily on RICO, money laundering, and asset forfeiture statutes to prosecute Russian crime syndicates. They consider these pieces of legislation as significant for combating organized crime activities as well as the structure of the criminal organizations.[64] Principal efforts to control Russian organized crime groups include the establishment of both domestic and international task forces and working groups aimed at dismantling these crime syndicates. Domestically, the FBI has set up *task forces* in areas such as New York City, New Jersey, Philadelphia, Chicago, San Francisco, Los Angeles, and Miami. Also, local police departments in major cities, including New York and Los Angeles, have set up Russian organized crime task forces.[65] In addition, the FBI is involved in international *working groups* concerned with Russian organized crime, including the Eurasian Organized Crime Working Group; the Central European Working Group at the International Law Enforcement Academy in Budapest, Hungary; and the Southern European Cooperative Initiative in Bucharest, Romania. The FBI is also involved in an international organized crime *task force* in Budapest, Hungary, aimed at combating Russian organized crime; currently, this is the only international task force aimed at combating organized crime in which the FBI is involved. The FBI has indicated that this international effort has been invaluable in developing international partnerships and intelligence, as well as expanding its international capabilities.[66]

Asian

Asian organized crime groups have had a presence in the United States since at least the early 1900s. However, there has been an increase in Asian organized crime since the 1990s.[67] Research indicates that there is not one unified Asian organized crime group; rather, there exist numerous crime syndicates, some more traditionally organized than others.[68] According to the FBI, traditional groups include Chinese triads from Hong Kong, Taiwan, and Macau, and the Japanese Yakuza. Less traditional groups include tongs, triads, and Asian street gangs such as the Big Circle and the Fuk Ching. Similar to a trend seen among Russian organized crime groups, an emerging trend seen among Asian crime syndicates is a willingness to cooperate across ethnic and racial lines if it is profitable for the enterprise. Asian organized crime groups derive most of their profits from trafficking in drugs—such as heroin—and people, but are also actively involved in other criminal activities, from money laundering, counterfeiting, and fraud to kidnapping and the theft of autos, software, and clothing. The FBI indicates that Boston, Chicago, Honolulu, Las Vegas, Los Angeles, New Orleans, New York, Newark, Philadelphia, Portland, San Francisco, Seattle, and Washington, DC, are examples of areas with a high prevalence of Asian organized crime.

U.S. law enforcement has relied heavily on RICO, money laundering, and asset forfeiture statutes to prosecute Asian crime syndicates. Similar to efforts aimed at combating Russian organized crime groups, U.S. law enforcement participates in domestic and international working groups aimed at combating Asian organized crime. Domestically, the Interagency Working Group on Alien Smuggling examines policy and investigative issues surrounding the smuggling of aliens and trafficking of women and children, including involvement of Asian organized crime groups in these activities. The FBI is also involved in international working groups concerned with Asian organized crime, including the FBI/National Police Agency of Japan Working Group, Interpol's Project Bridge, the International Asian Organized Crime Conference, the Canadian/United States Cross-Border Crime Forum, and the International Law Enforcement Academy in Bangkok, Thailand.[69]

Italian

The La Cosa Nostra (LCN) is the most prominent Italian organized crime group operating in the United States.[70] Within the LCN, there are five principal crime *families*.[71] The LCN is involved in an array of illegal activities, from gambling and loan sharking to drug trafficking and money laundering, that threaten American society.[72] Most members of the LCN operate in the New York metropolitan area, but there are also criminal operations in Boston, Chicago, Newark, Detroit, Philadelphia, and Miami.[73] La Cosa Nostra has been operating in the United States since the 1920s and still poses a threat today.

Early congressional and law enforcement efforts to control organized crime were aimed directly at controlling the illegal activities of the Mafia (LCN). As discussed earlier, these early congressional efforts involved enacting the 1968 Omnibus Crime Control and Safe Streets Act (P.L. 90-351) and the 1970 Organized Crime Control Act and RICO (P.L. 91-452), as well as the asset forfeiture and money laundering statutes. Civil RICO lawsuits have been particularly effective in purging the LCN from legitimate industries and unions, such as the Las Vegas gaming industry, the New York moving and storage industries, and the union representing truckers servicing JFK airport in New York.[74] In addition to federal RICO statutes, many states have also adopted RICO statues. Many believe that RICO has been the most powerful tool in combating La Cosa Nostra.[75] Despite these effective tools, the LCN remains a major organized crime threat to American society.

Balkan

The FBI identifies Balkan organized crime, and Albanian groups in particular, as among the most formidable organized crime groups today, as evidenced, in part, by an increase in Albanian-born individuals arrested in the United States.[76] Albanian organized crime groups emerged in the United States in the late 1980s and have evolved from being close knit families to allowing in outsiders with particular areas of criminal expertise. These groups are active in areas such as New York, Los Angeles, Las Vegas, Dallas, and Houston, to name a few. Balkan crime groups have been involved in various illegal activities such as gambling, extortion, robbery, counterfeit currency, drug trafficking, human smuggling, real estate fraud, money laundering, witness intimidation, and murder.

One emerging trend seen among Balkan organized crime groups is an increased cooperation with other organized crime groups—further evidence that Balkan organized crime is not just increasing, but expanding.[77] For example, the FBI has indicated that the LCN has partnered with Albanian organized crime in New York. There, the LCN is relying on the Albanians as their enforcers, and the Albanians have increasingly taken over some turf there that was previously dominated by the LCN.

Other Organized Crime Groups

The federal government recognizes threats from other organized crime groups that may not have the same notoriety as larger groups such as the LCN. For example, Middle Eastern criminal enterprises are primarily involved in organized theft, financial fraud, money laundering, and cigarette smuggling. Also, African crime syndicates—and particularly Nigerian groups—are involved in heroin trafficking, money laundering, and fraud (including insurance, bank, auto, healthcare, identity, and document fraud).

Of note, a trend among organized crime groups is that they begin by victimizing members of their own neighborhoods and ethnic communities, and then expand their illegal activities beyond these community lines. For example, in the 1920s Prohibition era, the Italian-American mafia began victimizing other Italians in the Five Points neighborhood of Little Italy in New York, before extending its activities to other neighborhoods of New York and the surrounding metropolitan area.[78] If this is indeed a common pattern across organized crime groups, then it is likely that emerging crime groups may expand their activities rather than restrict them to the areas in which they currently operate.

DOMESTIC IMPACT OF ORGANIZED CRIME

The U.S. Department of Justice Organized Crime Council,[79] chaired by the Deputy U.S. Attorney General, has identified eight strategic threats to the United States posed by international organized crime.[80] Of note, the term "international organized crime" includes not only those organized crime groups operating outside the borders of the United States, but within the U.S. borders as well. As mentioned earlier, the council noted that international organized criminals have and may penetrate the energy and other strategic sectors of the economy; provide logistical and other support to terrorists, foreign intelligence services, and governments; smuggle/traffic people and contraband goods into the United States; exploit the United States and international financial system to move illicit funds; use cyberspace to target U.S. victims and infrastructure; manipulate securities exchanges and perpetrate sophisticated frauds; corrupt or seek to corrupt public officials in the United States and abroad; and use violence or the threat of violence as a basis for power.

Former U.S. Attorney General Michael Mukasey outlined strategic goals in combating these threats. These goals continue to include

- targeting the largest organized crime threats,
- dismantling criminal organizations and removing their leadership,
- marshalling information from all available resources, and
- relying on all possible domestic and international tools and law enforcement partnerships.[81]

One specific goal of the Organized Crime Council that may be of particular interest to Congress is to "provide law enforcement with updated legislation and operational procedures needed to combat international organized crime."[82] Specifically, the Organized Crime Council indicated that laws and regulations should be expanded, updated, or modified to afford the government the abilities to investigate and prosecute organized criminals that affect American society from outside U.S. borders. This suggests that federal law enforcement currently may not have the extraterritorial jurisdiction or the most effective tools to combat the evolving organized crime threats to the United States. The section below provides a detailed discussion of some potential impacts of organized crime, followed by possible issues that Congress may consider.

Impact of Organized Crime on the Economy

Organized crime could weaken the economy with illegal activities (such as cigarette trafficking and tax evasion scams) that result in a loss of tax revenue for state and federal governments. This is particularly of issue given the current state of the country's economic health. Their fraudulent activities in the domains of strategic commodities, credit, insurance, stocks, securities, and investments could weaken the already-troubled financial and housing markets.

Money Laundering

Money laundering involves concealing the nature, location, source, ownership, or control of proceeds from an illegal activity or placing them back into further illegal activity.[83] The ill-gotten proceeds are laundered through a variety of methods to become "clean money." With the expansion of the Internet and increased globalization, the methods of money laundering continue to become increasingly complex and difficult to detect. The Financial Crimes Enforcement Network (FinCEN), under the Department of the Treasury, indicates that the routes for money laundering include banks, check cashers, money transmitters, businesses, and casinos. Money launderers use methods such as complex wire transfers, shell companies, and currency smuggling to hide their dirty money.[84]

Money laundering became a federal crime in the Money Laundering Control Act of 1986 (P.L. 99-570). It came to Congress's attention that organized criminals were camouflaging their proceeds, and Congress strengthened the federal criminal statues to better combat criminal organizations.[85] Recently, the scope of the money laundering statute has come under examination. Until more recently, the statute prohibited financial transactions of proceeds from illicit activities, but it did not define what constitutes "proceeds." The Supreme Court ruled in *United States v. Santos* that in the money laundering statute, the term "proceeds" refers to profits rather than gross receipts.[86]

Legislation enacted in the 111th Congress has since amended the money laundering statute. The Fraud Enforcement and Recovery Act of 2009, or FERA (P.L. 111-21), clarifies both the money laundering and international money laundering statutes. Namely, it indicates that "proceeds" includes gross receipts of illegal activities. Some experts have argued that expanding the predicate offenses for international money laundering could broaden the tools the federal government is able to rely upon when investigating and prosecuting organized crime that is increasingly crossing international lines. However, recently enacted legislation has not addressed these predicate offenses.

Cigarette Trafficking

Law enforcement agencies have also noted that criminal syndicates' participation in the trafficking of contraband cigarettes poses a significant threat to American society. A number of different organized crime groups are involved in cigarette trafficking. This illicit activity indirectly threatens the American economy and American communities. Cigarette smuggling leads to lost tax revenue.[87] Businesses, in turn, compensate by raising taxes for the consumer, ultimately placing the increased economic burden on the consumer.[88] Excessive economic burdens on the consumer are of particular concern now because of the current economic recession. Consequently, revenues that would assist in funding government programs are being illegally redistributed because of organized crime activities. Congress has repeatedly debated legislation to revise the Jenkins Act[89] to enhance reporting requirements for the sale of cigarettes and smokeless tobacco products as well as legislation to provide stronger penalties for smuggling such products.

Piracy and Counterfeiting

There is evidence that organized criminals are becoming increasingly involved in the production and distribution of counterfeit and pirated goods.[90] In Los Angeles County alone, Russian, Asian, Eurasian, and Lebanese organized crime groups are among those that have been involved in intellectual property rights crimes.[91] Industries targeted are broad, including the music and motion picture industries, clothing companies, luxury goods manufacturers, and the tobacco industry. The federal government has taken several steps so far in fighting these crimes. In fact, in March 2004, the Department of Justice created an Intellectual Property Task Force to combat the increase in intellectual property piracy and counterfeiting by organized crime groups. Also, the Office of the United States Trade Representative (USTR) has indicated that an Anti-Counterfeiting Trade Agreement (ACTA) is being formulated with other countries, including Australia, Canada, EU, Japan, Jordan, Korea, Mexico, Morocco, New Zealand, Singapore, Switzerland, and the United Arab Emirates. According to the USTR, one benefit of the ACTA is that it will help combat the piracy and counterfeiting that is an "easy source of revenue for organized crime."[92]

Counterfeit currency is another example of a domain in which many organized crime groups are involved. Asian organized crime groups in Los Angeles and New Jersey have been linked to the production of "supernotes," or fake $50 and $100 bills. This can not only lead to a loss in actual money (for those paid in the counterfeit currency), but it can damage the value of the U.S. dollar.[93] Some experts and policy analysts have suggested that one possible legislative option to help counter the involvement of organized crime in piracy and counterfeiting may be to expand the organized crime and money laundering statutes to include large-scale piracy and counterfeiting tied to other criminal activities.[94]

Organized Crime and Terrorists

In addition to concern surrounding the many industries in which organized criminals operate, both analysts and policymakers have expressed concern about the potential nexus between organized crime and terrorism. The principal distinction authorities make between organized crime groups and terrorist groups is motivation. Money motivates organized crime, and ideology motivates terrorism. Because of this fundamental difference, the National Intelligence Council expects that between now and 2020:

> [T]he relationship between terrorists and organized criminals will remain primarily a matter of business, i.e., that terrorists will turn to criminals who can provide forged documents, smuggled weapons, or clandestine travel assistance when the terrorists cannot procure these goods and services on their own. Organized criminal groups, however, are unlikely to form long-term strategic alliances with terrorists.

> Organized crime is motivated by the desire to make money and tends to regard any activity beyond that required to effect profit as bad for business. For their part, terrorist leaders are concerned that ties to non-ideological partners will increase the chance of successful police penetration or that profits will seduce the faithful.[95]

Despite the difference in motivation for organized crime and terrorism, the linking element for the two is money. Terrorist organizations may obtain funding from criminal acts, similar to organized crime groups. Also, terrorist organizations may launder these funds, similar to criminal organizations.[96] One example of a domain in which both organized criminals and terrorists may both benefit monetarily is piracy. Although there is currently less evidence of terrorist involvement in piracy, this business is a high-profit, low-risk activity, attractive to both criminals and terrorists.[97]

Even if organized crime groups and terrorist organizations do not form long-term alliances, the possibility of short-term business alliances may be of concern to citizens and policymakers alike. The FBI indicates that although it has not yet had a case of organized crime groups working directly with terrorists, the possibility exists, and it continues to be watchful for this nexus. Because organized criminals are monetarily motivated, the FBI believes that these criminals would be inclined to work with terrorists if offered sufficient funds.[98]

Although there are few reported instances of organized crime groups *actually* aiding terrorists, there are reported instances of international organized criminals *conspiring* to provide support to terrorist organizations. One such instance is Viktor Bout, an international arms trafficker who has been charged with conspiring to sell weapons to the Revolutionary Armed Forces of Columbia (FARC).[99] As mentioned earlier in this report, federal law enforcement distinguishes between organized crime groups and drug trafficking organizations. Although there are no reported instances of organized crime groups directly working with terrorists, there are reported instances of "narco-terrorism," or terrorism funded through the proceeds of drug trafficking; the Liberation Tigers of Tamil Eelam, members of Hizbollah, and the Al-Qaida network are all examples of terrorist groups with close ties to drug trafficking.[100] GAO reports that U.S. officials are concerned with the threat in Eurasia of the links between terrorist organizations and organized crime, and trafficking in persons and drugs.[101] With the prevalence of drug trafficking in the United States (via drug trafficking organizations as well as via organized crime groups that also have a hand in drug trafficking), policymakers may question (1) to what extent there is a nexus between domestic organized crime and terrorism and (2) what measures will most effectively combat both terrorism and organized crime.

POTENTIAL ISSUES FOR CONGRESS

The evolving nature of organized crime, as discussed, presents several issues that Congress may wish to consider. One issue is whether the tools that Congress has provided the federal government with to investigate and prosecute domestic organized crime—namely RICO, money laundering, and asset forfeiture statutes—are still effective tools to combat today's threats from organized crime. As evidenced by proposed legislation, Congress is considering clarifying and expanding these statutes so as to better equip the federal government to fight organized crime.

Federal Organized Crime Resources

Policies exist that allow federal law enforcement to investigate and prosecute organized crime groups. What may not fully exist, however, are the monetary and personnel resources to effectively combat organized crime—evidenced by a decrease in FBI agents used to investigate organized crime matters and in FBI organized crime case openings.

As previously discussed, in FY2004, the FBI utilized about 35% fewer agents on organized crime matters than it did in FY2000. Agent utilization on organized crime matters also declined by over 15% between FY2005 and FY2009. The FBI has recognized that prioritizing counterterrorism and counterintelligence cases affects resources available to criminal investigations and that targeting the most significant threats will allow criminal investigative resources to be used most effectively. FBI Director Robert Muller testified to the need for restoring resources to the FBI's criminal programs, which include organized crime.[102] Efforts—both administrative and congressional—can be made to this effect in several ways. One congressional option may be to increase overall funding available to the FBI and other federal law enforcement agencies that may be experiencing a decrease in resources dedicated to more traditional crime fighting matters, including organized crime. If these resources are then administratively allocated to criminal programs, organized crime agent utilization could potentially be more closely aligned with agent allocation without taking resources away from higher priority areas. Another congressional option may be to provide directed funding for organized crime matters. This option could ensure that any increase in funding intended to be directed toward criminal programs or organized crime matters would be utilized in those domains.

Yet another policy option may be to decide that the existing resources dedicated to organized crime are sufficient, given the limited financial resources available under the federal budget and given the national priority of combating the threats from terrorism. If, on the other hand, more funding were available or if the link between organized crime and terrorism were more direct, the case for reevaluating the funding directed toward organized crime might be stronger. However, considering the current budget constraints and priorities, some may consider existing organized crime funding as adequate.

Multilateral Crime Fighting

The federal government is already involved in several multilateral efforts—with state and local agencies as well as with international allies—to combat organized crime. With respect to working with domestic state and local law enforcement agencies, federal law enforcement agencies have formed joint task forces, some that target a variety of organized crime groups and some that target specific criminal organizations. Several of these task forces were outlined in previous sections of this report. Some analysts have suggested that despite the benefits of multilateral crime fighting, potential jurisdictional issues may arise. As organized crime groups have expanded their activities beyond state and even national lines, so has the responsibility for combating organized crime expanded. There exists a clear line between state and federal jurisdiction for prosecuting crimes. However, jurisdiction over agency responsibility for investigating cases may at times be unclear. This may be due in part to overlapping agency responsibilities and may also arise from the complexity of the cases investigated. For instance, an organized crime case with a drug component may fall under the jurisdiction of both the FBI and the DEA, potentially causing confusion on which agency would take the lead on such cases.

An issue that may become more visible than the issue of domestic law enforcement coordination is that of international law enforcement coordination. By ratifying the United Nations Convention Against Transnational Organized Crime in 2005, Congress took a step in working with foreign governments and law enforcement agencies to combat organized crime. Specifically, this Convention provided the framework for international cooperation by requiring mutual legal assistance between countries in fighting organized crime, as well as by requiring extradition for those organized criminal offenses outlined in the Convention. These provisions enhance the United States' ability to combat international organized crime and work with countries where there was no previous mutual assistance arrangement already in place.[103]

As organized crime becomes increasingly transnational, so may the need for international organized crime working groups, task forces, and law enforcement cooperation. The benefits of international cooperation and partnerships are twofold. U.S. law enforcement can extend its expertise and capabilities to assist overseas law enforcement combat organized crime. Partnering with international law enforcement will develop the intelligence needed to support domestic investigations of organized crime.[104] However, one of the challenges, as expressed by federal law enforcement, is the increased time required to conduct international investigations.[105] Among the various effects that this may have on investigations, organized crime groups may be inadvertently afforded a longer time to conduct their illegal activities, potentially affecting a greater number of victims or increasing the magnitude of damage to the victims. A second challenge relating to international investigations may arise from the domestic practice that federal prosecutors are involved at all stages of organized crime cases. When investigations are conducted abroad, the involvement of prosecutors may not be as consistent.

In addition to law enforcement collaboration with foreign nations, Congress has given the federal government extraterritorial jurisdiction to investigate and prosecute individuals who criminally violate U.S. interests abroad (P.L. 99-399).[106] This legislation was directed at combating terrorist acts against the United States, and thus the extraterritorial jurisdiction does not necessarily cover all crimes committed by organized crime groups. The increasingly transnational nature of organized crime as well as the potential for a nexus between organized crime and terrorism—as suggested by some analysts—may lead policymakers to question whether and/or how to extend this extraterritorial jurisdiction beyond the crimes currently covered with the practical and diplomatic challenges that such an approach may entail.

Potential Organized Crime Nexus with Terrorism

Some experts have indicated that the lines between organized crime groups and terrorist organizations may become increasingly blurry.[107] Even if organized crime groups and terrorist organizations do not form "long-term strategic alliances," as suggested by the National Security Council,[108] the links between organized crime and terrorism may still be significant. The council suggests (as does the FBI), however, that organized criminals and terrorists may ally for business purposes. Both criminal and terrorist organizations depend on money; organized criminals are profit-driven, and terrorists—though ideology-driven—need money and goods to finance their operations. It has been suggested that organized crime groups may cooperate with terrorists if the business alliance is profitable.

Some experts have cited potential additional areas of overlap between organized crime groups and terrorist organizations. For example, the language school that provided some visas for the 9/11 hijackers is also reported to have provided visas for prostitutes of a human trafficking ring.[109] There have also been instances of terrorist organizations drawing on the structure and activities of organized crime groups as models for structuring their organizations and financing their operations. Drug trafficking, for instance, has been one of the most profitable activities for both organized crime groups and terrorist organizations. Other illegal activities include human trafficking, weapons trafficking, endangered species trafficking, art and antique theft, counterfeiting, and credit card fraud.[110]

Because there may be overlap between organized crime groups and terrorist organizations in terms of their criminal activities and funding sources, some analysts have argued that combating organized crime is central to combating terrorism.[111] Congress therefore may consider the potential nexus between organized crime and terrorism when addressing the nation's security and determining the appropriate allocation and utilization of resources, as well as effective information sharing and interagency cooperation, as discussed above.

End Notes

[1] U.S. Department of Justice, "Remarks prepared for delivery by Attorney General Michael B. Mukasey on International Organized Crime at the Center for Strategic and International Studies," press release, April 23, 2008, http://www.usdoj.gov/ag/speeches/2008/ag-speech

[2] Ibid. The Organized Crime Council began meeting in 1970 and continued through 1993. When former Attorney General Michael Mukasey reconvened the Council in 2008, this was the first time it had met in 15 years.

[3] Department of Justice, Office of the Inspector General, Audit Division, *The External Effects of the Federal Bureau of Investigation's Reprioritization Efforts*, Audit Report 05-37, September 2005, p. 73. This statement is based on statistics from the FBI alone, not including other federal law enforcement agencies. The FBI is the federal law enforcement agency most involved in investigating organized crime matters.

[4] James O. Finckenauer, "Problems of Definition: What is Organized Crime?" *Trends in Organized Crime*, vol. 8, no. 3 (Spring 2005), pp. 63-82.

[5] According to the FBI, there are four main Italian organized crime groups operating in the United States: the Sicilian Mafia (from which the LCN was formed), the Camorra or Neapolitan Mafia, the 'Ndrangheta or Calabrian Mafia, and the Sacra Corona Unita or United Sacred Crown. The term "Mafia" tends to be an encapsulating term referencing all of these groups.

[6] Federal law enforcement tends to refer to organized crime groups as distinct from drug trafficking organizations (DTOs) or gangs. Therefore, this report does not include specific discussions of DTOs or gangs. For more information on DTOs (Mexican DTOs, in particular), see archived CRS Report R40582, *Mexico's Drug-Related Violence* , by June S. Beittel. For more information on gangs, see CRS Report RL34112, *Gangs in Central America*, by Clare Ribando Seelke; CRS Report RL34233, *The MS-13 and 18th Street Gangs: Emerging Transnational Gang Threats?*, by Celinda Franco; and archived CRS Report RL33400, *Youth Gangs: Background, Legislation, and Issues*, by Celinda Franco.

[7] RICO is codified at 18 U.S.C. § 1961-1968.

[8] As defined in 18 U.S.C. § 1961, an "'enterprise' includes any individual, partnership, corporation, association, or other legal entity, and any union or group of individuals associated ... although not [necessarily] a legal entity," and a "'pattern of racketeering activity' requires at least two acts of racketeering activity" to occur within 10 years of one another for a criminal organization to be prosecuted for racketeering. Racketeering is defined as any number of violations, including an act or threat involving murder, kidnapping, gambling, arson, robbery, bribery, extortion, or dealing in a controlled substance. See 18 U.S.C. § 1961 for a comprehensive list of the predicate offenses for racketeering.

[9] Frank Browning and John Gerassi, *The American Way of Crime* (New York: G.P. Putnam & Sons, 1980), p. 53.

[10] U.S. Congress, House Government Operations, Legal and Monetary Affairs, *Federal Effort Against Organized Crime: Report of Agency Operations*, committee print, 90th Cong., 2nd sess., June 1968.

[11] Congressional testimony in 1963 by Joseph Valachi—a prominent member of the LCN Genovese crime family— shed light on the true extent of the LCN network. Joseph Valachi was the first Mafia member to publicly affirm the existence of a criminal organization such as the LCN. In 1963, he testified before the Permanent Subcommittee on Investigations of the Senate Committee on Government Operations. For text of his complete testimony, please see U.S. Congress, Senate Committee on Government Operations, Permanent Subcommittee on Investigations, *Organized Crime and Illicit Traffic in Narcotics*, 88th Cong., 1st sess., September 25, 1963.

[12] Task Force on Organized Crime, *Task Force Report: Organized Crime: Annotations and Consultants' Papers*, The President's Commission on Law Enforcement and Administration of Justice, Washington, 1967, p. 14.

[13] From remarks by Rep. Dante B. Fascell, Chairman, in U.S. Congress, House Committee on Government Operations, Subcommittee on Legal and Monetary Affairs, *The Federal Effort Against Organized Crime. Part 1*, 90th Cong., 1st sess., April 5, 1967.

[14] From remarks by Fred M. Vinson, Jr., Assistant Attorney General, Criminal Division, Department of Justice, in U.S. Congress, House Committee on Government Operations, Subcommittee on Legal and Monetary Affairs, *The Federal Effort Against Organized Crime. Part 1*, 90th Cong., 1st sess., April 5, 1967.

[15] For this analysis, CRS used the data referenced in the U.S. Congress, House Committee on Government Operations, Subcommittee on Legal and Monetary Affairs, *The Federal Effort Against Organized Crime. Part 1*, 90th Cong., 1st sess., April 5, 1967. Convictions carry a greater burden of proof than indictments, and thus are more difficult for prosecutors to obtain. While the raw numbers of both indictments and convictions were on the rise, the *proportion* of indicted individuals who were later convicted decreased; this may suggest that organized crime was perhaps growing at a rate faster than the criminal justice system was able to handle.

[16] Task Force on Organized Crime, *Organized Crime: Report of the Task Force on Organized Crime*, National Advisory Committee on Criminal Justice Standards and Goals, Washington, 1976.

[17] U.S. Congress, Senate Committee on the Judiciary, *Organized Crime Control Act of 1969*, report to accompany S. 30, 91st Cong., 1st sess., December 16, 1969, S.Rept. 91-617.

[18] The LEAA administered federal funding for state and local law enforcement agencies, educational programs, research, and crime initiatives. It is no longer in existence and has since been succeeded by the Office of Justice Programs (OJP).

[19] The Omnibus Crime Control and Safe Streets Act was later amended by the Violent Crime Control and Law Enforcement Act of 1994. This amended Act addressed organized crime in that it expressed the sense of the Senate that "the United States should encourage the development of a United Nations Convention on Organized Crime." Five years later in 1999, the United Nations began developing a Convention against Transnational Organized Crime. The Omnibus Crime Control and Safe Streets Act was also amended by the Electronic Communications Privacy Act (ECPA) of 1986 (P.L. 99-508), which substantially revised Title III and related provisions. For more information on the ECPA, see CRS Report 98-326, *Privacy: An Overview of Federal Statutes Governing Wiretapping and Electronic Eavesdropping*, by Gina Stevens and Charles Doyle.

[20] Remarks from Sen. John L. McClellan, U.S. Congress, House Judiciary, No. 5, *Organized Crime Control*, 91st Cong., 2nd sess., May 20, 1970.

[21] Remarks from John N. Mitchell, Attorney General of the United States, U.S. Congress, House Judiciary, No. 5, *Organized Crime Control*, 91st Cong., 2nd sess., May 21, 1970.

[22] 18 U.S.C. § 3521. Although the foundation for the Witness Security Program was authorized by the Organized Crime Control Act of 1970, the program was established under Part F of Chapter XII of P.L. 98-473.

[23] RICO is codified at 18 U.S.C. § 1961-1968. For more information on RICO, please see CRS Report 96-950, *RICO: A Brief Sketch*, by Charles Doyle.

[24] See Howard Abadinsky, *Organized Crime*, 7th ed. (Belmont, CA: Wadsworth, 2003).

[25] See 18 U.S.C. § 1961 for a comprehensive list of the predicate offenses for racketeering. Offenses include—but are not limited to—crimes such as murder, kidnapping, gambling,

arson, robbery, bribery, extortion, dealing in obscene matter, dealing in a controlled substance or listed chemical, counterfeiting, theft from interstate shipment, embezzlement from pension and welfare funds, embezzlement from union funds, fraud and related activity in connection with identification documents or access devices, mail fraud, wire fraud, financial institution fraud, procurement of citizenship or nationalization unlawfully, obstruction of justice or criminal investigations, tampering with or retaliating against a witness, false statements or forgery in application and use of a passport or other documents, peonage, slavery, trafficking in persons, interference with commerce, and laundering of monetary instruments.

[26] Federal Bureau of Investigation, "Move Over, Mafia: The New Face of Organized Crime," press release, February 13, 2009, http://www.fbi.gov/page2/feb09/organizedcrime_021309.html.

[27] For more information on forfeiture, see CRS Report 97-139, *Crime and Forfeiture*, by Charles Doyle. Forfeiture comes in two forms: civil and criminal. Both result in the confiscation of property derived from or used in criminal activities. Criminal forfeiture is confiscation accomplished as part of the prosecution of the property owner. Civil forfeiture is accomplished through a civil proceeding ordinarily brought against the property involved in the illicit activity.

[28] Money laundering is codified at 18 U.S.C. § 1956. The Money Laundering Control Act is Subtitle H of Title I of the Anti-Drug Abuse Act of 1986. For more information on the federal money laundering statutes, see CRS Report RL33315, *Money Laundering: An Overview of 18 U.S.C. 1956 and Related Federal Criminal Law* , by Charles Doyle.

[29] In addition to the legislative efforts to control organized crime, there have been other national efforts aimed at assessing the activities of organized crime in the United States and providing recommendations for curbing its impact on society. Examples of advisory groups tasked with assessing the status of organized crime include the National Advisory Committee on Criminal Justice Standards and Goals (Organized Crime Task Force of 1976), the President's Commission on Organized Crime that met from 1983 through 1986, and the Organized Crime Council that met from 1970 to 1993. These groups have consistently concluded that organized crime remains a significant threat.

[30] Carrie Johnson, "Obama Team Faces Major Task in Justice Dept. Overhaul; Goal is to Restore Confidence in Law Enforcement Actions," *The Washington Post*, November 13, 2008, p. A02, Suburban Edition.

[31] U.S. Department of Justice, "Remarks prepared for delivery by Attorney General Michael B. Mukasey on International Organized Crime at the Center for Strategic and International Studies," press release, April 23, 2008, http://www.usdoj.gov/ag/speeches/2008/ag-speech

[32] See the Department of Justice, Organized Crime and Racketeering Section website at http://www.usdoj.gov/criminal/ links/ocrs.html.

[33] Because the FBI is the federal law enforcement agency leading the fight against organized crime, much of the discussion on federal crime control efforts in this report refers to the FBI. The examples used in this report, therefore, do not provide a comprehensive view of the federal efforts against organized crime.

[34] The FBI identifies organized crime threats on its website at http://www.fbi.gov/hq/cid/orgcrime/aboutocs.htm.

[35] From remarks by Chris Swecker, Acting Executive Assistant Director Law Enforcement Services, Federal Bureau of Investigation in U.S. Congress, House Committee on Homeland Security, Subcommittee on Management, Integration, and Oversight, *9/11*

Reform Act: Examining the Implementation of the Human Smuggling and Trafficking Center, 109th Cong., 2nd sess., March 8, 2006.

[36] While task forces tend to focus on investigating crimes, working groups tend to focus on discussing various threats and developing strategies to counter the threats.

[37] See the Federal Bureau of Investigation, Minneapolis Division Field Office website at http://minneapolis.fbi.gov/ taskforces.htm#organized_crime.

[38] An example of one such task force is referenced in: Federal Bureau of Investigation, "Pedro D. Ruiz Named SAC of New York Field Office's Intelligence Division," press release, September 19, 2007, http://www.fbi.gov/pressrel/ pressrel07/ruiz091707.htm.

[39] See the Department of Justice, Organized Crime and Racketeering Section website at http://www.usdoj.gov/criminal/ links/ocrs.html.

[40] United Nations Office of Drugs and Crime, *United Nations Convention Against Transnational Organized Crime and the Protocols Thereto*, United Nations, New York, 2004.

[41] INTERPOL is the largest international police organization, composed of 187 member countries. It facilitates international law enforcement cooperation, primarily through maintaining secure global police communication systems, operating data services and databases for police, providing operational police support, and promoting police training and development. For more information on INTERPOL, see http://www.interpol.int/.

[42] The USNCB transmits, responds to, and executes requests for international law enforcement cooperation in which the United States is involved. For more information on the USNCB, see http://www.usdoj.gov/usncb/.

[43] From remarks by Grant D. Ashley, Assistant Director, Criminal Investigative Division, Federal Bureau of Investigation, in U.S. Congress, Senate Committee on Foreign Relations, *Combating Transnational Crime and Corruption in Europe*, 108th Cong., 1st sess., October 30, 2003.

[44] Department of Justice, Office of the Inspector General, Audit Division, *The External Effects of the Federal Bureau of Investigation's Reprioritization Efforts*, Audit Report 05-37, September 2005, p. 73.

[45] Ibid., p. 14.

[46] The specific number of agents allocated to and actually utilized on organized crime cases is not publically available after FY2004. For this reason, CRS is unable to determine the current relationship between agents allocated to and agents utilized on organized crime matters.

[47] U.S. Department of Justice, "Remarks prepared for delivery by Attorney General Michael B. Mukasey on International Organized Crime at the Center for Strategic and International Studies," press release, April 23, 2008, http://www.usdoj.gov/ag/speeches/2008/ag-speech

[48] Department of Justice, Office of the Inspector General, *Follow-up Audit of Federal Bureau of Investigation Personnel Resource Management and Casework*, Audit Report 10-24, April 2010, p. iv, http://www.justice.gov/oig/reports/FBI/a1024.pdf.

[49] Department of Justice, Office of the Inspector General, Audit Division, *The External Effects of the Federal Bureau of Investigation's Reprioritization Efforts*, Audit Report 05-37, September 2005, pp. 74-75.

[50] From remarks by Robert S. Mueller III, Director, Federal Bureau of Investigation, in U.S. Congress, Senate Committee on Appropriations, *Commerce, Justice, Science, and Related Appropriations for FY2008*, 110th Cong., 1st sess., April 26, 2007, p. 305.

[51] Department of Justice, Office of the Inspector General, *Follow-up Audit of Federal Bureau of Investigation Personnel Resource Management and Casework*, Audit Report 10-24, April 2010, pp. 26-27, http://www.justice.gov/oig/reports/FBI/a1024.pdf.

[52] U.S. Department of Justice, Office of the Inspector General, Audit Division, *The External Effects of the Federal Bureau of Investigation's Reprioritization Efforts*, Audit Report 05-37, September 2005, pp. 73-75, http://www.usdoj.gov/oig/reports/FBI. CRS calculated the number of cases per agent based on the number of agents reported to be working on organized crime matters and the number of organized crime cases reportedly opened for FY2000 and FY2004. More recent data on organized crime case openings is not publicly available.

[53] The specific number of agents working on organized crime cases is not publically available after FY2004. For this reason, CRS is unable to determine whether the workload of agents working organized crime cases has fluctuated from the FY2004 level.

[54] See the Bureau of Justice Statistics flowchart illustrating case flow through the criminal justice system at http://www.ojp.usdoj.gov/bjs/largechart.htm.

[55] Committee on Law and Justice, National Research Council, *Transnational Organized Crime: Summary of a Workshop*, ed. Peter Reuter and Carol Petrie (Washington: National Academy Press, 1999), pp. 1-2.

[56] National Intelligence Council, *Global Trends 2025: A Transformed World*, NIC 2008-003, November 2008, p. 1, http://www.dni.gov/nic/PDF_2025/2025_ Global_Trends_ Final_Report.pdf.

[57] As mentioned, drug trafficking organizations (DTOs) are considered by DOJ and the FBI as separate from organized crime groups. Although many organized crime groups are involved in drug smuggling, trafficking, and distribution— among various other crimes—DTOs' *primary* involvement is drugs. For more information on the U.S. policy and efforts to combat drug trafficking, see CRS Report RL32352, *War on Drugs: Reauthorization and Oversight of the Office of National Drug Control Policy*, by Mark Eddy.

[58] The FBI identifies organized crime threats on its website at http://www.fbi.gov/hq/cid/orgcrime/aboutocs.htm.

[59] For purposes of this discussion, the term *Russian organized crime* refers to both Russian and Eurasian crime groups operating in the United States. The FBI and other experts also reference the combination of Russian and Eurasian crime groups under an umbrella term. See, for example, James O. Finckenauer and Jay Albanese, "Organized Crime in North America," in *Handbook of Transnational Crime and Justice*, ed. Philip Reichel (Thousand Oaks, CA: Sage, 2005), pp. 439-456.).

[60] U.S. Congress, House Committee on International Relations, *Threat from International Organized Crime and Global Terrorism*, 105th Cong., 1st sess., October 1, 1997.

[61] Russian crime groups in Russia have a more hierarchical structure than those groups operating in the United States. These groups, such as the Vory V Zakone, or "thieves-in-law," exhibit a structure more similar to the Italian Cosa Nostra. See Alexander Sukharenko, "The Use of Corruption by 'Russian' Organized Crime in the United States," *Trends in Organized Crime*, vol. 8, no. 2 (Winter 2004), pp. 118-129. Also see James O. Finckenauer and Jay Albanese, "Organized Crime in North America," in *Handbook of Transnational Crime and Justice*, ed. Philip Reichel (Thousand Oaks, CA: Sage, 2005), pp. 439-456.

[62] From remarks by Grant D. Ashley, Assistant Director, Criminal Investigative Division, Federal Bureau of Investigation, in U.S. Congress, Senate Committee on Foreign Relations, *Combating Transnational Crime and Corruption in Europe*, 108th Cong., 1st sess., October 30, 2003.

[63] These are the cities in which the FBI has set up special investigative units dedicated to investigating Russian organized crime.

[64] Federal Bureau of Investigation, "Inside the FBI: Organized Crime," press release, February 13, 2009, http://www.fbi.gov/inside/archive/inside021309.htm.

[65] James O. Finckenauer and Jay Albanese, "Organized Crime in North America," in *Handbook of Transnational Crime and Justice*, ed. Philip Reichel (Thousand Oaks, CA: Sage, 2005), pp. 439-456.

[66] Federal Bureau of Investigation, Remarks prepared for delivery by Robert S. Mueller, III, Director, Federal Bureau of Investigation, 10th Anniversary of ILEA Budapest, Budapest, Hungary, May 12, 2005, http://www.fbi.gov/pressrel/ speeches/muller051205.htm.

[67] Glenn E. Curtis, Seth L. Elan, and Rexford A. Hudson, et al., "Transnational Activities of Chinese Crime Organizations: A Report Prepared under an Interagency Agreement by the Federal Research Division, Library of Congress," *Trends in Organized Crime*, vol. 7, no. 3 (Spring 2002), pp. 19-57.

[68] Ko-Lin Chin, *Chinatown Gangs: Extortion, Enterprise, Ethnicity* (New York: Oxford University Press, 2000).

[69] Federal Bureau of Investigation, Organized Crime: Asian Criminal Enterprises, http://www.fbi.gov/hq/cid/orgcrime/ asiancrim.htm.

[70] According to the FBI, there are four main Italian organized crime groups operating in the United States: the Sicilian Mafia (from which the LCN was formed), the Camorra or Neapolitan Mafia, the 'Ndrangheta or Calabrian Mafia, and the Sacra Corona Unita or United Sacred Crown. The term "Mafia" tends to be an encapsulating term referencing all of these groups.

[71] The five principal crime families that make up the LCN are the Bonanno, the Colombo, the Genovese, the Gambino, and the Luchese families.

[72] Other principal threats that the LCN poses to American society are labor racketeering, political corruption, extortion, theft, bribery, kidnapping, fraud, counterfeiting, infiltration of legitimate businesses, murders, and bombings.

[73] James O. Finckenauer, *La Cosa Nostra in the United States*, International Center, National Institute of Justice, 2007, http://www.docstoc.com/docs/416307/La-Cosa-Nostra-in-the-Unites-States—2000.

[74] Frank J. Marine, Organized Crime and Racketeering Section, United States Department of Justice, Washington, District of Columbia, USA, "The effects of organized crime on legitimate business," *Journal of Financial Crime*, vol. 13, no. 2 (2006), pp. 214-234.

[75] James B. Jacobs, Christopher Panarella, and Jay Worthington, *Busting the Mob: United States v. Cosa Nostra* (New York: New York University Press, 1994).

[76] John DiStasio, "International Organized Crime Center," *United States Attorneys' Bulletin*, vol. 51, no. 5 (September 2003), pp. 2-6.

[77] Clint Williamson, "Balkan Organized Crime: The Emerging Threat," *United States Attorneys' Bulletin*, vol. 51, no. 5 (September 2003), pp. 42-48.

[78] *World Encyclopedia of Organized Crime*, ed. Jay Robert Nash (Dallas: Zane Publishing, 1995).

[79] The Organized Crime Council includes leaders from nine federal law enforcement agencies: the Federal Bureau of Investigation; the U.S. Drug Enforcement Agency; the Bureau of Alcohol, Tobacco, Firearms and Explosives; the U.S. Immigration and Customs Enforcement; the U.S. Secret Service; the Internal Revenue Service; the U.S. Postal Inspection Service; Diplomatic Security; and the U.S. Department of Labor, Office of the Inspector General.

[80] Organized Crime Council, *Overview of the Law Enforcement Strategy to Combat International Organized Crime*, U.S. Department of Justice, April 2008. In this Strategy, the Organized

Crime Council uses the broad term *international organized crime* to include organized crime in the United States. Former U.S. Attorney General Michael Mukasey has underscored the inclusion of domestic organized crime under the umbrella term of international organized crime, citing the globalization of crime and of groups with member around the world (including the United States). See U.S. Department of Justice, "Remarks Prepared for Delivery by Attorney General Michael B. Mukasey on International Organized Crime at the Center for Strategic and International Studies," April 23, 2008, http://www.usdoj.gov/ag/speeches/2008/ag_speech_080423.html.

[81] U.S. Department of Justice, "Remarks Prepared for Delivery by Attorney General Michael B. Mukasey on International Organized Crime at the Center for Strategic and International Studies," April 23, 2008, http://www.usdoj.gov/ag/speeches/2008/ag_speech

[82] Organized Crime Council, *Overview of the Law Enforcement Strategy to Combat International Organized Crime*, U.S. Department of Justice, April 2008, pp. 14-15.

[83] Money laundering is codified as a federal crime at 18 U.S.C. § 1956.

[84] See the Overview of Law Enforcement on the FinCEN website at http://www.fincen.gov/law_enforcement

[85] For more information on the money laundering discussions in Congress preceding the Money Laundering Control Act of 1986, see U.S. Congress, Senate Committee on the Judiciary, *Money Laundering Legislation*, Hearing on S. 572, S. 1335, and S. 1385, 99th Cong., 1st sess., October 29, 1985, S.Hrg. 99-540.

[86] "Supreme Court Narrows Scope of Money-Laundering Statute," *Criminal Justice Newsletter*, July 2008, pp. 1-3.

[87] Some experts have estimated that cigarette smuggling leads to about $40 million in lost tax revenue annually for governments around the world. For more information, see Framework Convention Alliance, "How big was the global illicit tobacco trade problem in 2006?," Prepared for the Second Session of the Conference of the Parties to the WHO FCTC, Bangkok, Thailand, June 30–July 6, 2007, http://www.fctc.org/dmdocuments/fca-2007-cop-illicit-trade-howbig-in-2006-en.pdf.

[88] U.S. Congressman Bobby Scott, "Prevent All Cigarette Trafficking Act of 2008," press release, September 9, 2008, http://www.bobbyscott.house.gov/index.php?option=com_content&task=view&id=346&Itemid=89.

[89] The Jenkins Act requires anyone that sells and ships cigarettes (to anyone except a licensed distributor) across a state line to provide monthly reports of these sales to the buyers' state tobacco tax administrators. It is codified at 15 U.S.C. § 375-378.

[90] U.S. Government Accountability Office, *Intellectual Property: U.S. Efforts have Contributed to Strengthened Laws, but Significant Enforcement Challenges Remain*, GAO-05-788T, June 14, 2005, http://www.gao.gov/new.items/d05788t.pdf. Counterfeit and pirated goods are those that are either fake copies or copies that have been reproduced without authorization.

[91] From remarks by John C. Stedman, Lieutenant, Sheriff's Department, County of Los Angeles, before the U.S. Congress, Senate Committee on Homeland Security and Government Affairs, *Counterfeit Goods: Easy Cash for Criminals and Terrorists*, 109th Cong., 1st sess., May 25, 2005, p. 8. Intellectual property rights (IPR) include copyrights, trademarks, trade secrets, and patents.

[92] Office of the United States Trade Representative, *Anti-Counterfeiting Trade Agreement (ACTA)*, August 4, 2008, http://www.ustr.gov/assets/Document_Library/Fact_Sheets/2008/asset_upload_file760_15084.pdf?ht=.

[93] Todd Bullock, "Narcotics, Counterfeiting Help Fund North Korea, U.S. Says: Senate hearing discusses Pyongyang's criminal operations," *America.gov*, April 26, 2006, http://www. america.gov/st/washfile-english/2006/April/ 20060426135925tjkcollub0.8716699.html.

[94] Gregory F. Treverton, Carl Matthies, and Karla J. Cunningham, et al., *Film Piracy, Organized Crime, and Terrorism*, RAND Corporation, Safety and Justice Program and the Global Risk and Security Center, 2009, http://www.rand.org/ pubs/monographs/2009/ RAND_ MG742. pdf.

[95] *Mapping the Global Structure*, National Intelligence Council, Report of the National Intelligence Council's 2020 Project, Based on consultations with nongovernmental experts around the world, Washington, D.C., December 2004, p. 96.

[96] Angela Veng Mei Leong, "Criminal Finance: Money Laundering and Terrorist Financing," in *The Disruption of International Organised Crime: An Analysis of Legal and Non-Legal Strategies* (Burlington, VT: Ashgate Publishing Company, 2007), pp. 29-67.

[97] Gregory F. Treverton, Carl Matthies, and Karla J. Cunningham, et al., *Film Piracy, Organized Crime, and Terrorism*, RAND Corporation, Safety and Justice Program and the Global Risk and Security Center, 2009, http://www.rand.org/ pubs/monographs/2009/ RAND_MG742. pdf.

[98] Pat Milton, "FBI Worries About an Osama-Sopranos Link," *Associated Press*, October 1, 2006, http://www.redorbit.com/news/general/676652/fbi_worries_about_an_osamasopranos_link/ index.html.

[99] Organized Crime Council, *Overview of the Law Enforcement Strategy to Combat International Organized Crime*, U.S. Department of Justice, April 2008, p. 3.

[100] Ibid.

[101] U.S. General Accounting Office, *Combating Terrorism: Interagency Framework and Agency Programs to Address the Overseas Threat*, GAO-03-165, May 2003, http://www.gao.gov/ new.items/d03165.pdf.

[102] From remarks by Robert S. Mueller III, Director, Federal Bureau of Investigation, in U.S. Congress, Senate Committee on Appropriations, *Commerce, Justice, Science, and Related Appropriations for FY2008*, 110th Cong., 1st sess., April 26, 2007, p. 305.

[103] From remarks by Bruce Swartz, Deputy Assistant Attorney General, Criminal Division, U.S. Department of Justice, at U.S. Congress, Senate Committee on Foreign Relations, *Hearing on Law Enforcement Treaties: Treaty Doc. 107-18, Inter-American Convention Against Terrorism; Treaty Doc. 108-6, Protocol of Amendment to the International Convention on the Simplification and Harmonization of Customs Procedures; Treaty Doc. 108-11, Council of Europe Convention on Cybercrime; Treaty Doc. 108-16, U.N. Convention Against Transnational Organized Crime and Protocols on Trafficking in Persons and Smuggling of Migrants*, 108th Cong., 2nd sess., June 17, 2004, pp. 29-37.

[104] Examples of international law enforcement partnerships can be found on the FBI's website at http://www.fbi.gov/ hq/cid/orgcrime/lcnindex.htm#pantheon, http://www.fbi.gov/hq/ cid/orgcrime/asiancrim.htm, and http://www.fbi.gov/page2/feb09/organizedcrime_021309. html.

[105] U.S. Department of Justice, *The Electronic Frontier: The Challenge of Unlawful Conduct Involving the Use of the Internet*, A Report of the President's Working Group on Unlawful Conduct on the Internet, March 2000, p. Appendix B, http://www.usdoj.gov/ criminal/cybercrime/append.htm#B.

[106] See the Omnibus Diplomatic Security and Antiterrorism act of 1968, Title XII of P.L. 99-399. For more detailed information regarding the United States extraterritorial jurisdiction as

well as the specific crimes are included in this jurisdiction, see CRS Report 94-166, *Extraterritorial Application of American Criminal Law*, by Charles Doyle.

[107] Thomas M. Sanderson, "Transnational Terror and Organized Crime: Blurring the Lines," *SAIS Review*, vol. XXIV, no. 1 (Winter-Spring 2004), pp. 49-61.

[108] *Mapping the Global Structure*, National Intelligence Council, Report of the National Intelligence Council's 2020 Project, Based on consultations with nongovernmental experts around the world, Washington, D.C., December 2004, p. 96.

[109] Louise Shelley, "The Globalization of Crime and Terrorism," *Global Issues*, February 2006, pp. 42-45.

[110] Ibid.

[111] Ibid.

In: Organized Crime
Editor: Jason D. Camilleri

ISBN: 978-1-61324-012-0

Chapter 3

EXPERT WORKING GROUP REPORT ON INTERNATIONAL ORGANIZED CRIME*

John T. Picarelli

The opinions and conclusions expressed in this document are solely those of the authors and do not necessarily reflect the views of the U.S. Department of Justice.

AUTHOR'S NOTE

The group of experts that assembled in late January 2010 came well prepared to assess the existing research on international organized crime and suggest where the community should turn next. As the organizer and rapporteur for the group, I would like to thank the attendees for taking time out of their schedules and arriving so well prepared and ready to engage the issues. Without their willingness to engage in an open discussion and, at times, a frank critique of the state of knowledge of international organized crime research, this meeting would have never succeeded in the way that it did.

Please note that the expert working group met under the Chatham House Rule. The Rule states, "When a meeting, or part thereof, is held under the

* This is an edited, reformatted and augmented version of a National Institute of Justice Discussion paper NCJ 230846, dated June 2010.

Chatham House Rule, participants are free to use the information received, but neither the identity nor the affiliation of the speaker(s), nor that of any other participant, may be revealed." As such, no direct quotes or comments are associated with specific participants. A full list of the participants and the agenda is found at the end of this report.

For more on the National Institute of Justice and its work in the field of international organized crime, please consult our Web site:_http://www.ojp.usdoj.gov/nij/.

John T. Picarelli
Social Science Analyst International Center
National Institute of Justice

INTRODUCTION

In January of 2010, the International Center of the National Institute of Justice (NIJ) assembled international experts and practitioners to assess the state of research on international organized crime (IOC). Two recent developments made this an opportune time for a working group to engage in a robust and critical reflection. The first was an expansion of IOC research. Although the number of books, journal articles and reports on IOC have steadily increased in recent years, the ways IOC research has expanded in other ways made this a good time to call such a meeting. For example, IOC research now goes beyond the traditional disciplines of criminology and sociology to include anthropology, economics, political science, history and other academic disciplines. Moreover, scholarly examination of IOC has gone beyond description and has increasingly focused on critical issues, such as how to improve the scientific rigor of IOC research. Last, this research now uses a mixture of methodologies, including historical, experimental, quantitative, qualitative and case study designs and increasingly implements international or comparative research designs to expand the geographical breadth of studies.

Dovetailing with this growing interest in IOC research is an accelerating effort to develop new strategies to address the IOC threat in the United States. Although not limited to the U.S. Department of Justice (DOJ), the DOJ's efforts are indicative of how this effort is unfolding. In 2008, DOJ released the *Law Enforcement Strategy to Combat International Organized Crime*, which outlined steps to revise its efforts to address IOC. The Attorney General also reconvened the Organized Crime Council (AGOCC), an interagency body that coordinates Federal law enforcement activity against organized crime. In reconvening the AGOCC, which had not met for 15 years, the Attorney General asked that it oversee the implementation of the law enforcement strategy and directed it to focus more on the IOC threat. In 2009, DOJ continued to implement the law enforcement strategy with the formation of the International Organized Crime Intelligence and Operations Center (IOC-2). Through IOC-2, DOJ and other federal agencies are now able to marshal the resources and information of nine U.S. law enforcement agencies and numerous federal prosecutor offices nationwide.

The Expert Working Group (EWG) advanced NIJ's efforts to meet two goals. First, NIJ fostered a new level of cooperation between researchers and practitioners. Although the level of participation in the EWG is a measure of this new cooperation, so too are the number of contacts that have continued after the meeting. Second, NIJ has been able to identify promising agendas for the IOC research community and for federal practitioners. This report provides the IOC research community with suggestions from the research and practitioner communities that can help steer the direction of IOC research for years to come.

NIJ has tasked the EWG to explore seven areas of IOC research, using a three-part rubric consisting of the quality of existing research, the most promising research agendas, and the most problematic methodological or programmatic obstacles (see Appendix A). The first issue was to examine what what we know about IOC. The group conducted a summary of existing IOC research and assessed its general qualities and its gaps. The second issue was to probe what IOC research should be pursued? This led into an important discussion about the impact that suggested research agendas could have on policy and practice. Last, and most important, the question of how to accomplish such research was addressed. The group identified the most effective research methods, explored what data was needed, and named the barriers that would impede these studies as well as ways to circumvent or mitigate them.

The sections that follow summarize the discussion in each of these seven areas. The report concludes with a discussion of recurring themes from the meeting and a series of recommendations on how to proceed with IOC research. As the meeting was held using the Chatham House Rule,[1] none of

[1] For more information on Chatham House Rule, see http://www.chathamhouse.org.uk/about/chathamhouserule/.

the participants is named in this report, but their comments are recorded as accurately as possible.

THE VIEW OF PRACTITIONERS

The EWG opened with a general discussion of the requirements for research from the practitioner's perspective. This opened a dialogue between the stakeholders for research, primarily practitioners from various U.S. and foreign government agencies and the research community. Practitioners are stakeholders in the IOC research because they rely on research to inform their decisions on both IOC policy and programs. Yet practitioners are often unable to follow the trends and developments in the broader IOC research field, given the need to maintain expertise in interests that are often narrow (e.g., asset forfeiture or prosecutorial techniques). The relationship between research and practice is largely a paradox wherein practitioners maintain a narrow expertise in an IOC subfield in order to make well-informed decisions but researchers focus on the broader context to achieve a more comprehensive understanding of IOC. The key is to find a way to connect the researcher and the practitioner in a way that benefits both.

Beginning with a discussion of recent U.S. government initiatives against IOC, examples included AGOCC and other recent DOJ initiatives to refocus its efforts.[2] Since 2008, the AGOCC has resumed quarterly meetings and is focusing on IOC as the primary organized crime threat facing the United States. The discussion also covered the major topics of DOJ's *Law Enforcement Strategy to Combat International Organized Crime.*[3] This document lays out four priorities for the U.S. government in fighting IOC: marshalling information and intelligence on IOC, prioritizing and targeting the most significant IOC threats, using the widest range of tools against IOC, and dismantling entire IOC networks.

Another major topic during this session was the recently completed National Intelligence Estimate (NIE) on IOC. The NIE was the first comprehensive study of the threat of IOC to the United States in more than 15 years; it drew on the combined resources of the intelligence community, the

---

[2] For more on the AGOCC, its composition and its history, see http://www.justice.gov/ag/speeches/2008/ag_speech_080423.html.

[3] A public version of the strategy is found at http://www.justice.gov/ag/speeches/2008/ioc-strategy-publicoverview.pdf.

AGOCC and private experts. Although the full results of the NIE are classified, some of the public details were presented at the meeting. The NIE noted two broad trends: the role that globalization has played in transforming IOC, and the expanding networks and interconnections among different IOC groups.

The NIE characterized the threat from IOC across four broad categories. The first was the growing nexus between national governments and IOC, in some cases to the point where government and IOC organizations worked hand in hand. The concern is not only that government leaders are profiting from IOC but also that IOC groups are becoming an instrument of state power. Another NIE concern is the widespread corruption that is subverting the institutions of certain countries. The erosion of governance due to corruption in regions such as West Africa and Central America were of particular concern.

The NIE also explored the economic threat from IOC. Although the NIE mainly focused on the anti-competitive behavior of IOC and its impact on legitimate business activities, it also considered the impact of IOC on future global economic growth. The latter is all the more concerning because global economic growth is expected to be concentrated in emerging states that are particularly vulnerable to IOC. Thus, the threat to U.S. businesses from IOC is a worldwide threat and is not limited only to markets important to U.S. security interests. Another concern focused on the ability of U.S. business firms to compete globally, given how IOC penetration of businesses might skew these sectors. A final economic concern addressed in the NIE was IOC's growing involvement in markets that are considered strategic to U.S. security and well-being, such as energy and metals.

The NIE examined two IOC threats fueled by globalization: cybercrime and terrorism. Cybercrime has a multiplier effect on IOC, allowing it to inflict more harm on the global financial system and individual citizens than those crime groups that operate in a more traditional fashion. The NIE concluded that IOC is one of the most sophisticated perpetrators of cybercrimes, so understanding this linkage is of particular importance to governments. The NIE also explored the development of relationships between international criminal and terrorist organizations. Once a terrorist group forms a relationship with IOC, such as in drug trafficking, the terrorist group obtains access to a revenue stream that is hard for government actors to interrupt or eliminate. IOC therefore can serve as a lifeline to terrorist groups, especially when law enforcement puts pressure on terrorist groups and manages to dry up some of their funding.

Aside from the specific initiatives of the U.S. government, the practitioners in the EWG largely agreed that the partnership between government agencies and the research community was vital to their efforts to counter IOC. Research on IOC informs policy and program decisions made by practitioners (e.g., evaluation of counter-IOC tools for U.S. use). Practitioners also noted that IOC research regularly informed their deliberations on the AGOCC and in other venues. Some of the specific areas where they felt research could help improve policy and process included:

1. **Organizational structures:** What are the hierarchy, membership, compensation and governance of IOC groups? How do these structures vary across different IOC groups, and what accounts for this variation? What are the goals of IOC groups? What cultures and demographic groups are involved with IOC groups? What are the needs and services of IOC groups? How do these groups form networks across regions of the globe?
2. **Motivations:** What drives these groups? Are these groups only concerned with making money? What part does power or prestige play in IOC groups? How does this factor into convergence between criminal and other groups, such as the terrorist–crime nexus?
3. **Business model:** Do we understand the nature and types of business activity associated with IOC groups? How is it related to the maturity of the organization? Does the size of the organization matter? What economic or other environmental factors drive the organization? What is the impact of legitimate business on illicit business, and vice versa? How do the licit and illicit sides interface?
4. **Management and vulnerability:** What are the best measures to obscure the location of the proceeds from IOC? What financial products are most at risk? Given that some crime groups are more sophisticated than the institutions they target, how knowledgeable are these institutions about the risk of IOC groups? Do IOC groups handle their own money laundering? Does this vary by group, region or size?
5. **Role of government:** Precisely how do IOC groups work with governments? Are such groups purely external to government, or do they also infiltrate government in some way? To what extent does IOC mobilize government policy? To what extent does IOC use its assets to assist the government and, if they do, what is the motivator (e.g., money, personal relationships)? What is the primary means of probing into government–IOC collaborations?

6. **Harm:** What is the harm that flows from IOC? What is the economic harm caused by IOC groups? Why is it so bad if IOC infiltrates or creates a legitimate business? How do we quantify other impacts of IOC, such as human misery, public safety and threats to free commerce? How can we quantify what portion of losses due to cybercrime are attributable to IOC?

Practitioners also discussed some areas of special concern to their agencies. Smuggling and the illicit trade of goods, ranging from contaminated medicines to hazardous materials, was one topic raised. Another area of concern was the theft of intellectual property. Last, practitioners noted that they need researchers to provide them information to improve their performance and protection against IOC groups.

The discussion that followed the practitioners' presentations focused on prioritization. When researchers have been able to examine government-produced threat assessments, they were able to help practitioners see the larger picture and identify emerging and nontraditional threats from IOC. For example, one participant noted that their organization had witnessed a significant increase in the number of smaller IOC networks in recent years as well as the growing importance of cybercrime in cross-border forms of crime. Another participant noted the increasing importance of the real estate sector in both fraud and money laundering associated with IOC.

The other topic addressed at the end of this session focused on priorities for the private and other nongovernmental sectors. Given that IOC responds to opportunities to profit, researchers can focus on what opportunities exist for IOC to exploit. Put another way, what private sector activities are more vulnerable to crime and corruption than others? For example, how does the expansion of SMART cards impact the incidence of money laundering, fraud or corruption, if at all? In summary, exploring vulnerabilities and opportunities is a way to help the private sector set its priorities when countering IOC and also aid in law enforcement and other criminal justice responses to IOC.

Obstacles

One obstacle that was raised during the opening session was the flow of information between stakeholders and researchers. Many of the researchers recalled the difficulties they have had in obtaining information from stakeholders, including information that a reasonable person would assume is publicly available. Stakeholders generally agreed on the need to share data with researchers to establish a baseline of "scientific information documenting these areas," but they also noted the prohibitions against sharing information that was either classified or related to an ongoing investigation or case.

ACTORS

The next session focused on the actors associated with IOC. The EWG opened with a discussion of international criminal organizations and how are they organized. The EWG also focused on how other actors, especially legitimate or seemingly legitimate actors, facilitate or participate in IOC. The diversification of the criminal activities of international criminal organizations was a third topic, which included the degree to which crime groups focus on facilitating specific forms of crime such as documents fraud or money laundering. Last, the group examined how international criminal organizations learn, communicate with one another, recruit, and perform other maintenance and operational tasks. In summary, this segment sought to deconstruct how criminal organizations operate in order to identify the key gaps in our knowledge of them.

The group agreed that research on international criminal organizations is robust. The fact that the vast majority of definitions of IOC rely on organizational characteristics to segregate IOC from other forms of criminality suggests that organizational analysis is a primary lens in IOC research. Characteristics commonly found in IOC definitions include a continuing hierarchy of leadership roles, restricted memberships and specialization, rational forms of profit-seeking behavior, the use of force or the credible threat of force to obtain their goals, the corruption of public officials, and monopolies over licit or illicit markets. A different set of studies focuses on the place of international criminal organizations on a continuum of crime groups. Although the most easily recognized are large, formal and well-organized criminal groups, they occupy only one end of the spectrum. On the other end are smaller "Mom and Pop" organizations consisting of a handful of collaborators. The ability to operate across borders is not a function of size but rather is a trait exhibited in a number of different types of criminal organizations.

Thus, one of the first recommendations the EWG offered was to continue current lines of research on the organization of criminal groups. The group felt that conducting numerous studies would produce more rigorous results and would better identify trends. Participants further felt that researchers should focus on the organizations involved in more high-risk activities and markets before examining how individuals initially became involved with the crime groups. Focusing on high-risk activities would lead to the high-risk people operating those activities. Another suggestion was to focus on research into white-collar crime, which could identify why certain crimes require the establishment of more formal organizations as opposed to crimes committed through informal and ad hoc networks.

The EWG felt that there were gaps in the research on IOC organizations and certain areas needed further development, so they made a number of recommendations. One of the main recommendations was for researchers to focus on individual criminals entering crime groups as a way to discover new aspects of IOC. The group felt that IOC research needs to examine and "mine" the criminal careers of individuals, including the careers of those who failed at organized crime. Such basic research could lead to a number of important projects. One project could be to understand the relationship between individual criminals and the larger contexts within which they work, especially how offenders bridge distance and cultural differences by applying their special skills and being adaptable (e.g., foreign criminals operating in Russia vs. Russian criminals in their own country). Second, studies of individual criminals could evaluate accepted models of organized criminality for validity. For example, the notion of a strict diversification of criminal groups, especially international criminal organizations, is probably false because of the presence of the same individuals or criminal cliques in two or more of these groups. Studies of individuals could also help clarify the notion of internationally mobile offenders or "criminal entrepreneurs" who serve numerous purposes for international criminal organizations but remain a relative mystery beyond some anecdotal studies. Last, some participants felt that studies of former criminals who have "gone legitimate" and have become wealthy businessmen or oligarchs would be edifying if these individuals had truly left behind a life of crime.

Another recommendation for IOC research was to examine how groups organize to engage in specific forms of IOC. For example, to date, no researcher has explored the logistics of IOC, so practitioners do not have a systematic understanding of how crime groups move people around, communicate, or run other aspects of their multinational operations. Nor has research catalogued the attempts, successful or otherwise, of international criminal organizations to invest in (or capture) licit sectors of the economy. To this end, participants noted that any research detailing the relationships between crime groups and licit actors, such as businessmen and political leaders, would further clarify how corruption and protection of criminals are accomplished in IOC organizations.

Last, the EWG saw the need to consider sociocultural factors and their relationship to international crime groups. At a micro level, researchers could explore the degree to which society or culture influences an individual's decision to join these groups; perhaps a comparative study could be conducted to discover if reasons for joining are different across different international criminal organizations. Investigating what kinds of opportunities that IOC provides — to segments of society denied the ability to work or otherwise advance — could prove useful. On a more macro level, some societies or cultures are known to more easily tolerate the existence of these crime groups, but it not clear why. Participants suggested that studies could examine the conditions that make some states or other jurisdictions more vulnerable to criminal influences. Another related suggestion from the EWG was to map out and explore the formation of "covert spaces," which provide crime groups the opportunities to supplant government authority. Likewise, studies could focus on how IOC dismantles forms of governance that threaten crime groups while simultaneously constructing new forms of governance more tolerant of IOC. In general, practitioners noted that any studies that could identify how to engender positive forms of governance would have more of an impact on IOC than more generic studies of governance.

Obstacles

Overall, the EWG remained optimistic about completing much of the proposed IOC research. For example, a number of participants from both the research and practitioner communities noted the potential for sharing more data between law enforcement and the research community. The fact that researchers are active in this area means that there exist valid data collection and research methods for future research. Researchers can draw on a growing body of research in human trafficking and cigarette smuggling to improve their data sources, offender and victim interviews, criminal file analyses and intelligence data, all of which are accessible to researchers.

A number of concerns and potential obstacles were noted that researchers would need to address. The first concerned the data that researchers rely on; some participants noted that law enforcement information is limited to the actors who got caught. It is important that researchers recognize this limitation in the presentation of their results, especially because this is the main source of data for studies examining IOC actors. One suggestion was to improve access to structured data sets on IOC drawn from law enforcement agencies worldwide. However, such information is not always forthcoming because law enforcement agencies are reluctant to have their performance compared with others. Nevertheless, such data would prove useful, even if certain identifying markers, such as originating agency, were removed.

The EWG also noted the difficulty of conducting timely IOC research on actors and other aspects of IOC. Some participants noted that high-quality studies require more time and thus more support to complete. For example, conducting a proper harm assessment requires that the researcher deconstruct numerous concepts: the actors, the definition of success and failure, the logistical contexts, and so on. Researchers cannot complete harm assessments without addressing all of these points. Thus, such projects often start out with more basic research on the actors before they move into the more complicated study of the harm done. If the research environment is not conducive to sponsoring basic research, however, then it is unlikely that high-quality studies of harm from IOC will emerge.

As this was the opening session of the EWG, participants also made a number of recommendations that were of a more general nature for IOC research. First, the group felt that IOC research often lacks the details that practitioners require. Although there was a recognition that the complexity of studying IOC often precludes more granular studies of the issues, researchers were urged to strike a better balance between generalizability and practicality in the presentation of their results. One suggestion was for researchers to publish in both academic and professional journals, placing scholarly and theoretical works in the former and more granular and policy-oriented findings in the latter.

Second, the EWG also called for more comparative research on IOC. Several studies examine how IOC operates in a specific country or how criminals travel to conduct crime in other countries. However, IOC studies rarely examine the comparisons across cultures or countries, and how crime groups operate in their own countries versus the destination countries.

Third, the EWG noted that there is very little in the way of grand theory building in IOC research. Most studies of IOC remain limited to elements of their case studies or other data, which in turn limits the ability of researchers to generalize beyond certain sectors of IOC or regions of the globe. The group urged IOC researchers to commit to broader explanations of IOC that are rooted in theory.

Last, participants stressed the need to support the creation of a proper IOC research community that reflects the interdisciplinary nature of the work and of the EWG. This research community would foster more collaboration amongst researchers across borders and encourage younger scholars to continue the current research. Although some suggestions were offered on how to support this effort, the group felt this topic should be considered further at a future roundtable or other meeting.

National Security Issues

The EWG next considered the various intersections of IOC with national security. One intersection is between the nation-state and IOC. International criminal organizations are able to co-opt the nation-state processes to suit their own interests, and the state can also use international criminal organizations to advance their interests. Also considered were the various ways that IOC can be a security threat in different countries, not merely targeting "weak" ones but also having the capacity to work around countries' different criminal justice procedures and approaches to fighting IOC. Last to be discussed on this topic was the relationship between IOC and other malevolent actors, such as terrorist or insurgent groups, and how that factors into considerations of national security.

States, Society and IOC

Although existing research in this area was not as robust as research on IOC actors, the group found that two topics in particular had garnered the attention of researchers. The first was the relationship between IOC and governments. Research has demonstrated that this relationship was not simply one of corruption, although corruption is an important element. Rather, the relationships between international criminal organizations and governments need to be considered on a more complex level. Some in the EWG noted that both sides can benefit from such relationships, whereas others noted that the relationship represented a significant threat to countries. Addressing the latter, participants doubted that "state capture" was likely to happen, given the overwhelming strength of national governments. Yet, research has demonstrated that there are times when the national government can serve as the largest international criminal organization within a nation-state.

Governments have also used forms of organized crime, such as kidnapping, as a strategic weapon to maintain their control over society. One participant summarized this debate over the relationships between governments and IOC as "barbarians at the gate" versus "barbarians in the gate."

The EWG also cited research that supported the need to study the complex relationship between governments, societies and IOC on a global scale. It was noted that it is not just the relationship between IOC and governments that matters; how society fits into the equation also plays a role. In one European country, for example, organized crime appeared at times to be more powerful than the national government; however, recent reforms have subjugated the organized crime groups (but not eliminated them). Another European country has a long history of close ties between organized crime and different levels of government, in spite of an active social movement against organized crime and recent successful national campaigns against IOC. One participant discussed the impact that recent violence in a Latin American country had on the severing of ties between portions of the national government and IOC. In summary, the relationships between criminal organizations, states and segments of society are complex and hard to generalize across borders.

Turning to the need for research, the group arrived at a number of potentially promising research agendas. One was a comparative analysis that would identify which governments are more likely to collude with IOC. Research along these lines would naturally support policy choices designed to reduce or eliminate collusion between governments and IOC. For example, this research could demonstrate how governments adopt new social services or sequence the introduction of new economic policies to reduce the influence of IOC. Such a study could also demonstrate the need to link justice and "rule of law" programs more closely to socioeconomic programs and development. Last, this research could provide insights into how to balance interdiction campaigns — designed to slow the growth of organized crime — with social campaigns — designed to strengthen governance.

Another topic that the EWG felt warranted more research is the capacity of national governments to respond to IOC. Some participants felt it was important to learn if reduced government services in times of economic or budgetary shortfalls then lead to the formation or strengthening of ties between the society and IOC. This is especially true of cuts in criminal justice and banking agencies, given the recent allegations of fraud and abuse during the recent global economic crisis. Likewise, some participants wondered if it is always wise for states to suppress the illicit economies that might prove to be the only security for some segments of society. More studies are needed on how to build capacities such as police forces. Studies need to move beyond the imperative that "the government must act" and include recommendations on *how* the government must act. Last, some urged that researchers look for links between IOC and nongovernmental organizations, especially those NGOs that are crucial to governance practices within countries. Although little evidence suggests that this is a significant problem, it remains a yawning gap in the study of IOC and how it impacts on governance.

IOC, Terrorism and Insurgency

Another relationship the working group considered was that between IOC and either terrorist or insurgent groups. The group was largely disappointed with the research examining the links between IOC and terrorism. One participant offered that, on this topic, researchers "often view the world the way [they] want it to be, not the way it really is." Some participants built on this sentiment by noting that terrorist organizations do not have to work with crime groups in order to profit from organized crime. Research offers numerous examples where terrorist groups have appropriated the profit-making activities of organized crime without working directly with the criminal organizations (e.g., the drug-trafficking activities of FARC and Al-Qaeda in Mesopotamia).

The EWG was strongly in favor of further research in this area, given its potential impact on the criminal justice and national security policies of countries. Some recommendations for future research on the crime-terrorism interaction were proposed. Not surprisingly, one of the strongest recommendations was for more basic research detailing and cataloguing these relationships. Studies that document how specific criminal and terrorist organizations have collaborated and how terrorist groups engage in IOC would be very helpful. Participants also recommended that these studies clearly define organized crime and terrorism in order to conduct a critical appraisal of their relationships with one another.

Another area of interest was to examine how trust evolved in such relationships. Sometimes the relations between terrorist groups and criminals break down, leading to mistrust. Studies could explore how governments could exploit these opportunities. Moreover, research on how trust between criminal and terrorist actors relies on external facilitators could provide important information about how these relationships function. Facilitators who provide false documents, money-laundering services, or other support to malevolent actors could play an important role as neutral arbiters to stabilize situations where trust is an issue.

Last, the EWG noted that a broader literature exists on the economics of modern conflict, which can serve as a springboard for further study on how IOC interacts with insurgencies and with conflicts among warlords or on a national/regional level. Although the group felt that further research in this area is welcome, they recommended that scholars review these studies to glean more insights into the crime-terrorism linkages. Some participants wondered if this literature might also prove useful in establishing what role maritime piracy plays in the relationship between national/regional conflicts and IOC.

Obstacles

Members of EWG noted some potential pitfalls and obstacles to completing quality research in this area. They generally agreed with one participant's observation that the research community needs to beware of "policy-correct knowledge." Given the politically charged nature of this area of research, especially research examining the relationship between IOC and terrorism, researchers were urged to be mindful of how policy considerations might drive the research or presentation of the results. Many in the group felt this was more of a general caution, and one that was not limited to research on terrorism and IOC.

Another concern was the lack of multidisciplinary studies in this and other areas of IOC. The group felt that too many publications are addressed to only one academic discipline, and that not enough cross-fertilization between schools of thought had occurred. For example, political economists tend to publish in journals that cater to political scientists and economists, but criminologists do not tend to read these journals. Participants urged their colleagues to move beyond this artificial limitation and seek a more interdisciplinary approach by conducting broader literature reviews and presenting papers at academic conferences that cover more diversified subject matter.

Last, some of the participants noted that research in this area, among others, might require more specialized training (e.g., financial forensics or anti-fraud training). Researchers should consider how available specialized training might enhance their studies of IOC.

SMUGGLING

As one participant noted, most research on IOC is often a study of one or more forms of smuggling. Covering a diverse set of criminal activities, smuggling encompasses the illicit movement of contraband and also the unregulated or illicit movement of legal goods, stolen goods, and even people. During the discussion, the EWG focused on the different forms of smuggling and the causes of specific smuggling patterns. The group also examined the similarities and differences among various smuggling organizations.

The existing research on smuggling is well developed and breaks down into three main categories. First are studies of smuggling that have focused on individuals and organizations of various sizes, with data on ethnicity, country or region of origin, extent of organization, nature of expertise, methods used to cross borders, the scale of operations, and the nature and extent of ties between component parts of smuggling networks. Second are studies of smuggling as responses to market forces, with a particular focus on the scale and organization of markets for smuggled goods and persons. Such studies include the magnitude of smuggling flows and related revenues, the extent of global market harmonization versus regional integration, and forms of imperfect competition.

Last are studies that focus on the impact of socioeconomic and political contexts on smugglers. Topics include the opportunities and constraints created by:

- Patterns of criminalization and law enforcement, trade and financial liberalization.
- Immigration control policies and patterns of migration and refugee flows.
- Global and regional economic crises.
- Interstate or civil wars, insurgencies or terrorism.
- State fragmentation and collapse.

These research agendas have met varying levels of success but generally have helped identify patterns from the diverse organization of smugglers and markets. The studies have also explained these patterns through theoretically informed conceptual models and methodologies grounded in economics, criminology, sociology, anthropology and, more recently, political science. Last, historically grounded studies have emerged that have determined trend lines and watershed moments for different forms of smuggling. An extraordinarily rich historical literature on smuggling exists. One participant noted that the founder of Brown University, often revered as a patriot, was also revealed as a smuggler in some of these studies.

Yet the state of knowledge about smuggling remains narrow for two reasons. First, most studies tend to focus on a single commodity. Studies that compare two or more forms of smuggling would provide more robust and generalizable findings that practitioners require. Second, the published material on smuggling tends to reflect the priorities of wealthy countries and thus does not address how smuggling operates in poorer nations. One result of these observations is that studies of drug trafficking have dominated the research on smuggling. Moreover, within these studies of drugs, there is a selection bias toward hard drugs (e.g., cocaine and heroin) over soft or even legal drugs (e.g., prescription abuse) and a bias toward the violent dimensions of drug trafficking at the expense of the reality that drug trafficking is often low-profile and nonviolent.

Research Agendas

From an examination of the existing literature, the EWG arrived at a number of recommendations for future research. The group's main recommendation was for a research agenda that explored the actors, markets and contexts of smuggling, using a comparative approach across place, time and smuggling activities. Such an approach would benefit from the integration of new voices through fieldwork, workshops and multidisciplinary international research teams that facilitate access to local area experts. This approach could help practitioners to better understand existing and emerging smuggling patterns, such as the sudden increase in border tunnels not only between Egypt and Israel but also on the southwest border of the United States.

Comparative analysis across places, if conducted at the national level, would focus on how smuggling links the licit and illicit worlds. A focus on the transportation aspect of smuggling would provide a window into the variety of licit and illicit actors that can enter the transaction chain. This chain provides a more comprehensive picture of the market for smuggling and attendant business practices and also allows researchers to examine the choices that smugglers make to conceal goods or deceive inspectors. In summary, examining all of the actors and actions involved in smuggling provides a way to trace the transformation from a legal businesses to criminal activities.

The EWG also noted that comparing how smuggling operates across time is a fertile area for research. By overcoming the "presentism" in research that assumes smuggling is new and different in the current era, it is possible to produce medium- and long-term smuggling trends and to evaluate the effectiveness of anti-smuggling policies over time. In so doing, historical studies can demonstrate value for policymakers who must deal with smuggling in the present. For example, historical information seemed to indicate that smuggling from China to the United States required high levels of logistical sophistication, but more recent research has found that loosely connected entrepreneurs are the most frequent smugglers and are not part of large international criminal organizations. The implication for policymakers was that it is probably not beneficial for agencies to investigate one or two cases in the hope of finding a big network; rather, agencies should focus on the destruction of the smaller networks.

Studies should also examine how the nature of the commodity influences the smuggling venture. The EWG felt that such an approach would help move the research community beyond the current prominence of compartmentalized studies of single forms of smuggling. Because these studies focus overwhelmingly on drug trafficking and, to a lesser degree, human smuggling, this approach would also strengthen research efforts in other smuggling areas such as arms, stolen and counterfeit goods, or money. Last, this comparative approach would serve as another window on the complexity of smuggling operations. For example, narcotics and human smuggling studies have revealed that a loosely knit group of service providers are available to assist smugglers. Comparative studies would identify whether such structures exist for other forms of smuggling.

One last topic that arose during this session was regarding the merits of studying legalization as a policy for countering smuggling. Recent legislative initiatives and economic difficulties worldwide have led to serious discussions of the value of legalizing and regulating certain illicit goods. No agreement was reached on the value of such an approach, but it was noted that the evidence of such initiatives is mixed at best. For example, some countries have a tolerant approach toward the sex industry, but anecdotal evidence suggests that such policies might encourage sex trafficking. In sum, legalization was viewed as a complicated topic but worthy of further study, especially if researchers were to evaluate existing legalization programs.

Obstacles

The group noted four problems that can hamper research into smuggling and other aspects of IOC. The first was a pragmatic issue of data collection. Numerous studies of smuggling suffer from either a lack of data or a lack of quality in existing data. Creating new data sets and improving the quality of existing data are therefore important first steps in promoting studies of IOC. The second problem is that this field does not lend itself well to scholarly research. For example, institutional review boards (IRBs) serve an important function in academic research: the elimination of potential harm to interview subjects in proposed studies. In smuggling research, however, IRB staff can impede the process if they lack the expertise. Moreover, the group could not overlook the potential for harm to the researcher studying smugglers and smuggling practices, further reinforcing the need for experienced IOC researchers. Third, some noted that IOC research is sometimes not considered a legitimate area of inquiry by mainstream scholars, which can discourage younger scholars from studies in this field.

Last, the EWG returned to two impediments to IOC research in general. One impediment was the political ramifications of smuggling research. As noted in the discussion of legalization, smuggling specifically, but IOC in general, are politicized areas of research. Researchers must always be wary of engaging in the creation of "policy-correct knowledge" at the expense of a more critical or nuanced view of the subject matter. The other issue that arose was the lack of multidisciplinary studies of IOC in general. One participant noted that smuggling was an area that not many criminologists had yet explored and guessed that maybe only 10 scholars from the IOC field had engaged the topic. One of the key challenges of IOC research is to translate different activities into their economic value. To accomplish this requires knowledge from multiple disciplines. Scholars need to overcome the separation of disciplines as "silos of knowledge," which makes it difficult for scholars to collaborate across disciplines and move forward in their research.

Penetration of Economic Sectors and Critical Infrastructures

The EWG's attention next turned to the relationship between IOC and legitimate businesses — primarily how international criminal organizations are purchasing businesses or otherwise penetrating financial markets. Many stakeholders are concerned about IOC investments in critical infrastructures (e.g., rail and pipeline) or strategic materials (e.g., oil and metals) as well as the harm that IOC inflicts on economic sectors. A sound estimate of the harm that IOC inflicts financially on businesses would be helpful information for the stakeholders to have.

The group felt that the existing research in this area is thin. Very few detailed studies exist on IOC's interplay with legitimate markets; those that do tend to focus only on certain markets. For example, there have been very few studies on the influence of international criminal organizations on real estate markets, although the recent downturn in real estate has exposed some of these linkages through media reporting. Yet the participants presented examples of large, often multinational businesses under the control of international criminal groups, such as the Alfa Group case and the anti-Mafia campaign in New York City in the 1980s. Other participants noted that significant information already exists on how international criminal organizations invest in legitimate businesses, such as forming false corporations in U.S. jurisdictions. Participants also presented evidence of lawyers and other "facilitators" who act, wittingly or unwittingly, as go-betweens for international criminal organizations and legitimate businesses.

The evidence suggests that the relationship between international criminal organizations and legitimate commerce is a complex picture. Some international criminal organizations invest in businesses in order to garner licit profits, thus serving as passive sources of equity. Others are more active in their involvement, using their investments to negatively impact the operation of businesses and markets. For example, some reports note that businesses operating at the behest or under the influence of international criminal organizations engage in labor practices that the U.S. recognizes as predatory. Over time, these relationships can become quite complicated. For example, individuals who had reaped significant funds from IOC in the past and are now operating "clean" businesses might, or might not, continue to benefit from IOC. Indeed, participants discussed, at length, some historical comparisons between modern oligarchs and the robber barons of the 19th and early 20th centuries arose as a part of this discussion.

CORPORATE RAIDING

One area that is starting to garner more media reporting and academic studies is the practice of international criminal organizations colluding with government agencies to "raid" corporations. The evidence suggests that this is a growing problem in some countries, but not all countries. For example, one country has recorded 300 incidents annually with total losses totaling $40 million.

Corporate raiding is usually a three-step process. First, crime groups obtain the documents of control for a corporation. For example, a crime group can create a fake power of attorney between itself and the owner of the business and then file it so that it becomes official. The crime group can then bring a suit to freeze assets and use the judicial documents in their favor. The second step involves the crime group physically taking over the targeted firm, often by using a private security company to seize assets on the basis of legal documents the group obtained through earlier court proceedings. Finally, the crime group transfers the assets of a firm to a purchaser through a shell company.

From a research point of view, it is important to look at what happens when IOC enters legitimate sectors of the economy. International criminal organizations engaging in legitimate commerce often do not behave like other licit firms would; through their actions, they often pollute national and international legal systems. Such behavior is extremely pernicious because it empowers crime groups and turns victims of crime into defendants. Moreover, practitioners noted the difficulty of attacking this scheme because extortion is taking place within or through the legal system and because investigators have to dig through complicated legal documents and decisions to make the case.

There exist a number of crimes that are similar to corporate raiding. The first is *vexatious prosecution*, a scheme in which a criminal prosecution is brought for an improper purpose. Sometimes, these prosecutions are initiated by law enforcement, but third parties initiate these cases for business competition purposes. This form of extortion exploits ambiguities in regulations on goods and services and other laws. A second form of this scheme is called *intellectual property racketeering*, in which crime groups obtain the legal right to intellectual property for the purpose of extorting money. Crime groups either trademark a good and hold the mark until the legitimate mark holder pays money to get it back, or the criminal group obtains a patent for a minor innovation of an existing product and extorts the patent holder. In summary, corporate raiding and its variations serve as a primary way to link international criminal organizations, governments and legitimate firms.

Research Agendas

The group arrived at five recommendations for further study of how IOC and legitimate business interact. The first was to explore the impact of IOC on markets in a general sense. Researchers need to wade into this area and answer some basic questions. As one participant noted, this research would answer the classic question, "So what?" For example, a number of historical parallels were drawn between today's forms of "crony capitalism" in developing states and the evolution of the "Wild West" the United States in the 19th century. However, such comparisons rarely rely on a scientifically valid, comparative historical study when they conclude that such crony capitalism will evolve into some form of business that the rule of law governs.

Thus, even basic research could provide important information for practitioners and other stakeholders. Studies could focus on how IOC compromises the normal work of the market and how it threatens the countries in which it operates. Studies could also ascertain if legitimate businesses in a free market are shut out or disadvantaged because of IOC's presence in the market. Last, the group thought that not only do studies that focus on specific markets have merit but comparative studies across different markets also have merit. For example, one participant noted the importance of understanding how IOC has penetrated the real estate market, whereas others saw value in examining IOC's penetration of markets in different countries as a potential way of improving our understanding of state or economic failure.

Participants suggested that a second agenda be focused on identifying which firms or economic sectors are most at risk for IOC penetration. Participants were interested in knowing whether those firms and sectors where IOC can make the most money are also the ones most at risk. A similar concern was whether the level of regulation of economic sectors correlates with the risk of IOC penetration. Others noted that it is not only vulnerability that researchers should focus on but also capacity and intent. To accomplish this, researchers could consider the role of corporate social responsibility in relation to the role IOC plays in firms. Finally, researchers could explore the openings or opportunities for IOC to enter certain sectors of the economy. Studies could focus on the necessary level of resources needed to expand into an economic sector and on how financial tools, such as tax evasion and alternative sources of revenue, allow IOC to penetrate an economic sector.

Third, the group recommended that researchers examine a number of aspects of international criminal organizations to see if some are more likely than others to penetrate economic markets and firms than other crime groups. Because little is known about how international criminal organizations invest their funds, tracing their investment strategies in licit businesses and markets could yield some insights into which crime groups are more likely to invest in specific sectors (e.g., telecommunication firms). Likewise, researchers could plot international criminal organizations along measures of organizational attributes (e.g., maturity or illicit activities) to see the correlations with their approaches to investing in legitimate firms and economic sectors. The EWG was also interested in exploring who actually comes out ahead when IOC invests in or enters a business. Although anecdotal evidence suggests that criminal groups derive the most benefits, systematic studies might prove otherwise. One participant noted that the research on La Cosa Nostra and its dealings in the U.S. private sector might serve as an appropriate parallel to this sort of research.

The participants felt that these studies should not limit themselves solely to international criminal organizations but should also examine the role of third-party facilitators. For example, one participant felt that banks and other financial service providers that shield crime groups from "know thy customer" rules facilitate IOC. Researchers could explore how businesses voluntarily enter into willing relationships with crime groups or even engage in illicit activities themselves. Useful studies would include comparisons between firms that engage with IOC and firms that, through environmental or other factors, are attracted to getting involved with IOC.

The fourth suggested area of research was to examine how individuals within international crime organizations approach licit commerce and markets. One topic that most occupied the EWG in this discussion was how researchers might explore the historical analogy between the oligarchs of today and the robber barons of yesteryear; both either engaged directly in or worked alongside criminal organizations to accomplish their goals. Hindsight shows that some of the work of the robber barons was positive and that most of their activities were licit under the laws of the time. Comparative historical studies could further illuminate this observation and see if there are parallels with modern oligarchs. Other participants called for research to examine the role of government agencies in blocking the worst abuses of the robber barons; the growth of the progressive movement expanded this power of the state. Modern oligarchs rely on governments to largely favor them over social movements, often through corruption and illicit means. Finally, one participant noted that historical analysis appears to indicate that robber barons were multigenerational in nature. If confirmed, this interesting finding might prove more valuable in a comparative analysis on economic trends.

The EWG did not feel that the analysis of individuals was merely a historical one because questions remain about the relationship between IOC and oligarchs. Not all oligarchs had or currently have clear ties to criminal groups. A topic the group felt deserved more research was "reputational laundering," the process by which individuals are rendered legitimate and socially acceptable through their investments and charitable works without threatening their ties to ill-gotten gains or crime groups. Even though oligarchs and other members of the international business elite may appear clean, their close associates may be the links between the elites and the criminal organizations. One participant noted the potential utility of this research for policymakers and for creating incentives for individuals to leave crime groups. However, researchers would need to present their data carefully, as poor data can mistakenly implicate a legitimate businesspersons and hurt their businesses.

The topic of discussion regarding economic penetration was another call for more comparative research. Because the threat of IOC's involvement in licit markets differs across countries, researchers must determine how to compare IOC harm across countries and produce comparative research that yields swift analyses on how economic and market trends affect the impact of IOC. Some noted that certain segments of the economy, such as real estate, lend themselves to not only cross-national but also cross-regional analyses of vulnerability. Participants also noted that although the term *oligarch* is usually associated with Russia, the phenomenon is also prevalent in numerous other countries, so researchers should compare data across multiple countries when possible.

In summing up the session, participants expressed concern at the lack of urgency on the part of policymakers and other practitioners on this issue. One participant made this point by asking the hypothetical question for policymakers: Would they have approved of John Gotti buying large segments of General Motors or of large foreign firms, with clear ties to IOC, purchasing U.S. firms or strategic assets such as port facilities? The group felt this topic had a clear and direct link with national security concerns, but that the problem, according to one participant, was that no one agency was focusing on the big picture: how money flows, business trends, IOC and other elements are converging globally. The group agreed that this research would inform policymakers about how IOC enters global business markets and would lead to improved financial and regulatory policies.

Obstacles

During this session, the group remarked on another obstacle to research: the role of definitions. How do researchers across disciplines and across countries define IOC? Definitions are important for any study and are especially important for any comparative studies of IOC. For example, if definitions of IOC are rooted in rule-breaking activity (i.e., conducting criminal activities), then how does one account for the fact that states can change the rules? Along those lines, some in the group wondered if "penetration" was the right word because it suggests that something outside of the market intervenes. Rather, some group members suggested examining the economic activity itself to see where the legal environment provides opportunities for crime.

PIRACY AND CYBERCRIME

The group next turned to two topics that researchers are starting to explore. The first was the degree to which international criminal organizations are involved in the piracy of intellectual property, goods and other products. The second topic, given the importance of computers and information networks in these activities, was how cybercrime and IOC overlap.

In general, the view of the group was that these are both areas with a small but growing body or research. Starting with cybercrime, the group noted the increasing importance of the Internet to our society and our systems of governance. In many ways, the Internet is a hostile environment because it is not yet governed by the rule of law. One participant likened it to an arms bazaar and brought forward some research findings to demonstrate the point. Whereas intrusions into U.S. government networks have increased 40 percent in recent years, only 1 percent were successfully prosecuted. Furthermore, 98 percent of bank heists are now conducted online. Losses from cybercrime totalled $1 trillion in 2009. Recent studies have documented a 200 percent increase in intrusions into U.S. government networks in 2010; some attacks cost as much as $6.3 million in losses on a daily basis.

Moreover, research is demonstrating the emergence of a mature, service-based economy for computer hacking and for the development and deployment of malicious software. Online criminal activities that profit from this development include intellectual property theft, the sale of malicious software code (e.g., cyberweapons) and cyberextortion. Criminal groups exist online but, unlike their terrestrial cousins, they are ephemeral and do not meet in person. Studies have demonstrated that the typical online criminal group consists of at least five people: a reconnaissance person, a person to exploit code to load into programs, a data miner, a money launderer, and an original coordinator associated with IOC. Given that 108 countries have cyberattack capabilities that can be deployed against the United States, this is likely to remain an area of concern for IOC stakeholders in the years to come.

The EWG next discussed the state of research on intellectual property theft, a challenging field that researchers have only begun to explore in depth. The piracy of intellectual property covers a wide scope and includes the theft of DVDs, software, pharmaceuticals, cigarettes, airplane parts, counterfeit goods and other items. The group characterized the piracy of intellectual property as a low-risk, high-profit environment. There is a low entry cost because products are cheap, and distribution costs remain low because of well-developed IOC networks linked to distributors. On the demand side, the theft of intellectual property is fueled by the large consumer demand for luxury goods. Estimates are that between 7 percent and 10 percent of pharmacy products are pirated and that piracy captures roughly 9 percent of overall world trade; however, researchers do not agree on the reliability of these numbers.

Little research has been conducted on the harm done as a result of intellectual property piracy. In terms of harm to the consumer, research has tried to distinguish between deceptive piracy, where the buyer thinks they are purchasing legitimate merchandise, and nondeceptive piracy, where the buyer knows the product is not legitimate. Deception often proves more harmful, such as when counterfeit medication proves ineffective. However, nondeceptive piracy might also prove harmful in an economic or even a social sense.

It is difficult to estimate the total loss due to intellectual property theft. As firms have developed better ways to describe losses, estimates of intellectual property theft have generally been in the billions of dollars annually. For example, a confidential informant told investigators that counterfeit cigarettes are a much more profitable and less risky business than drugs. Quantifying the size of the problem is all the more difficult because of the decentralized structure of intellectual property theft. With the advent of the Internet, other technology improvements and improved shipping mechanisms, distribution channels have multiplied.

The global recession has exacerbated cybercrime and intellectual property theft for two reasons. First, many information technology professionals lost their jobs during the recession, creating a new talent pool from which to recruit malevolent actors. Second, the rise of offshore outsourcing of intellectual property development, especially software development, has increased the systemic risk of falling victim to cybercrime and intellectual property theft. One participant noted that this is especially true for online hosting companies, which store an increasing share of the global data of individual and corporate technology users.

RESEARCH AGENDAS

Given the basic level of research in these areas thusfar, the EWG's recommendations have focused mainly on how to improve our overall knowledge of cybercrime and the piracy of intellectual property. Starting with cybercrime, participants suggested that basic research was the best strategy for research in the short term. The group felt that studies describing the relationship between IOC and cybercrime would provide stakeholders a baseline from which to evaluate existing assumptions about cybercrime. For example, such studies could evaluate stereotypes about hackers being young and more ideologically motivated. As one participant noted, anecdotal evidence suggests that hackers "are not just a bunch of crazy kids."

Participants had three suggestions on how research might proceed beyond basic descriptive studies. First would be studies that explore how international criminal organizations utilize cybercrime as a form of information gathering and counterintelligence. Participants cited recent media reports that national governments are using cybercrime to collect information from their adversaries. It is not a big leap to assume that international criminal organizations are using cybercrime for the same ends. Participants felt that this research might also confirm the existence of "virtual Mafias" and other forms of IOC that exist purely in cyberspace.

A participant suggested that another research topic in this area would be the impact that promotion of "hacker culture" has on international criminal organizations. For example, one country's government offered high school students the opportunity to compete in contests to prove their hacking skills, and the winners were quickly moved into government cyberwarfare agencies. The hacker culture has led to unintended consequences, however. For example, it is estimated that this same country has 150,000 "hacker crews." Thus, studies that explore how hacking and other forms of cybercrime operate in different cultural contexts can help improve our knowledge of its relationship to IOC.

The third topic of discussion on cybercrime research focused on its links to the financial sector. Participants pointed out that cybercrime can facilitate money laundering and cybercriminals may engage in counterfeiting that supports IOC. Research could also focus on responses to the threat of financially related cybercrime. For example, studies could examine how governments can put tracers on hubs of hacker services and online money launderers to improve investigations and responses to IOC. Another research suggestion was to explore how the use of existing asset forfeiture laws can be applied to online money laundering.

Turning to the piracy of intellectual property, the EWG again noted the need for basic research on how it operates and how it links to IOC. One participant suggested that researchers determine the profits from piracy, categorized by the type of intellectual property being pirated. Such research would require the compilation of "real dollar figures," not estimates, for stakeholders to better target the perpetrators of intellectual property theft and define their probable involvement with IOC. In addition, this research could explore the ways in which national and local governments sanction the counterfeiting of intellectual property and how this might encourage the involvement of international criminal organizations.

Further research is also needed that provides details about the market for pirated intellectual property. Several participants asked for more research on the societal and cultural contexts of piracy and research to pinpoint the role of international criminal organizations as opposed to more local or national criminal activity. Finally, some noted that research on Internet piracy of intellectual property needs to focus on its impact on the normal flow of money and assets, which would improve stakeholders' ability to target piracy and international criminal organizations.

Last, researchers could examine the legal codes pertaining to the piracy of intellectual property. Given that the majority of enforcement measures against intellectual property violations are rooted in civil as opposed to criminal law, participants felt this was an area ripe for exploration. In particular, some participants felt that a public–private model might prove most advantageous for fighting intellectual property theft. Others noted the need to examine how changes in legal codes and regulations might impact the market for pirated intellectual property. Finally, one participant noted the need to examine sentencing for intellectual property theft, suggesting that lenient sentences from judges reinforced the "high profit, low risk" model found in other forms of IOC.

Several participants noted the need to educate the public about the piracy of intellectual property, although they were not suggesting it as a research topic per se. One participant noted that piracy of intellectual property is another problem that "we cannot prosecute or litigate our way out of." Educational programs based on solid research would have a better chance of reducing demand and, in turn, reducing piracy better than law enforcement campaigns alone would accomplish. A good model of piracy would also provide the public with an accurate picture of the harm associated with piracy. Much of the research suggested in this session would help to arrive at this model.

Obstacles

Some obstacles to researching cybercrime and piracy arose during this session. A participant noted that researchers have to be cautious about data supplied by industry sources and about working with firms too closely on both issues. Given the obvious investment that firms have in protecting their interests, their threat assessments have proven to be inflated at times. Another challenge for researchers is that hackers are often not the "usual suspects" but are often people with no prior criminal records who do not fit the usual profile of organized criminals. Therefore, some models from criminology and other disciplines may not prove as useful.

CORRUPTION

Corruption is a topic that is integral to the understanding of IOC but is largely studied outside the context of IOC. Given the many sources of corruption and the numerous ends that corruption serves, the study of corruption covers a broad range of academic literature. For this discussion, the EWG limited their discussion to the degree to which IOC drives corruption, as opposed to responding to corruption, and specific ways that corruption facilitates IOC. The experts also explored the forms of corruption that are most often associated with IOC. One expert previewed the discussion by noting that the participants should understand the more explicit connection between IOC and corruption and not just explore IOC as a conduit for corruption.

The EWG noted that there is already significant research from which to build. In particular, the group noted a number of statistical studies that examine the link between corruption and crime. For example, the International Country Risk Guide has a number of questions on corruption and serves as a private database that correlates closely to the database maintained by Transparency International.[4] Another example is a study in Tanzania that evaluated the impact of raising government salaries as an anti-corruption strategy. The group concluded that corruption was an area with enough existing research to recommend that researchers move beyond basic research to applied research.

Overall, the EWG recommended seven broad areas for future research on corruption. The first was for researchers to explore different definitions of corruption and how they relate to IOC. A participant noted that, even though definitions differ, the World Bank's definition contains a useful phrase, "abuse of public position for private gain," that describes the linkage of IOC to corruption. However, the group also noted that previous research has shown that corruption is a symptom and not a cause to be targeted.

Second, the EWG felt that the research on corruption's links to IOC needed to "bring in the state" more often. Some noted that studies should better explain how countries create opportunities for corruption through leadership, legal codes, regulations or other mechanisms. For example, some states have restrictive laws that promote corruption, whereas others with bank secrecy laws create havens for corrupt officials to bank their ill-gotten gains. Other participants noted the need to look at fragile, weak, post-conflict and even post-disaster countries and examine how they create openings for corruption by having no oversight mechanisms. Regardless of the type of country, the group agreed that more research was needed on how corruption binds political leaders and international criminal organizations. Also needed within this research is an examination of the role of facilitators of corruption: not just corrupt officials but also the lawyers, notaries, bankers, businessmen, and others who serve as the connection or catalyst for corruption in government.

Participants next recommended that researchers examine the underlying causes of corruption to better understand its relationship to IOC. For example,

---

[4] See http://www.prsgroup.com/ for more on the ICRG and its methodology.

smuggling tends to involve corruption because cross-border movement either requires or greatly benefits from payoffs to officials to facilitate or guarantee the illicit movement. Such payouts to lower level officials often beget payoffs to higher level officials, which in turn can impact the legitimacy of a national government and breed other forms of criminality such as protection rackets. However, participants noted that researchers should move beyond the simple "corruption begets crime, and vice versa" argument and become more precise in how corruption is linked to specific illicit activities. Another suggestion was to construct a flow chart of corruption targets to differentiate the purpose of bribing high-level officials from the purpose of bribes to lower level civil servants. Such research can help stakeholders draft regulations and other legislation that mitigates rather than encourages corruption.

The fourth recommendation was for researchers to conduct comparative research across numerous countries. As one participant noted, examining corruption across multiple countries allows for a better understanding of how it links IOC to leaders and others. Comparative studies can model the link between corruption and IOC by using cultural, historical, social, political and other points of comparison. A participant provided an example in a study of three neighboring countries in which one housed a corrupt ruling elite that left no room for IOC to flourish, a second contained a merger of politicians and military officers that used IOC to promote its own ends, and a third had a sizeable organized crime presence but was still able to undertake reforms of government structures. Given their close proximity, the study was able to draw out how different policy choices and other factors led to the formation of corrupt links between governments, elites and IOC.

The EWG also noted that researchers need to evaluate structural factors. For example, many participants noted the conventional wisdom that corruption is more likely to occur when public officials are not adequately paid. However, recent scholarship has demonstrated that this does not stand up to scrutiny, as studies of corruption on the U.S. border with Mexico have borne out. The role of the cultural context was a major topic of interest to many participants. Some felt that although it may appear that a "culture of corruption" exists in some countries, other participants interjected that what may appear as cultural forces may actually be the result of a structural failure of government to provide services to its citizens. In other words, bribery becomes the only way to get anything done and thus serves as a practical reality but not a particularly cultural attribute.

The EWG also called for research on how to mobilize society against corruption and IOC. The group felt that civil society is a crucial element in fighting corruption and IOC, noting examples such as the outrage against the Mafia in Italy in the 1980s and 1990s, which led to a major crackdown against corruption and IOC. Researchers could explore how governments might provide assistance to countries in such a way as to incentivize and promote a culture of lawfulness. Alternatively, researchers might explore how society benefits from IOC. Some participants also noted that business associations should be brought into the conversation as a part of civil society.

Last, the group felt that studies of corruption need to provide specific information and guidance to governments. Some were concerned that policy and technical assistance can be based on possibly false assumptions; they see research as the potential cure. Studies could use available experiential data and criteria for measuring corruption to compare salaries and the incidence of corruption both explicit and transparent. Studies are also needed that evaluate potential legislation for its impact on corruption, for example, avoiding ambiguous statutes that can lead to corruption. Another potential topic for research is the way in which corruption operates in the judiciary, and whether it is easier to bribe a judge or a jury. Studies that target specific aspects of corruption can provide more guidance for policymakers and other stakeholders.

ADDITIONAL ISSUES

Even though some topics arose frequently during the two days of discussion (e.g., the need for comparative studies), two warranted a separate discussion. The first was the need for evaluations of a broad range of tools that government agencies use in the fight against IOC. The other topic deserving separate attention is the need to measure harm from IOC and to convey it to the public in a more meaningful way.

Evaluation Studies

A number of participants observed that credible evaluations of IOC programs and policies were lacking. The most significant concern was the presentation of "best practices" when, in fact, no evaluation study had validated the practice. Although many of these programs have met with success, defined in terms of arrests or convictions, deeper evaluations of the programs should seek to identify the reasons for their success, how to further improve the programs, and how these programs might work in other countries. This last aspect of evaluation studies, referred to as *transferability*, is important given the significant need for technical assistance to improve international cooperation against IOC.

One participant discussed how their agency used evaluation to identify best practices. The agency started with a definition of IOC and sought to understand how it impacted the local community. They next developed a plan to collect intelligence on IOC that would yield information on the active IOC groups in the country. After two years, the agency had collected information on about 500 criminal groups. The agency used this information to implement some programs (e.g., combating money laundering) but also used it to evaluate the effectiveness of these programs on the basis of their impact on known criminal groups.

Participants had a number of specific recommendations for evaluation studies. One noted the need to identify the potential, unintended consequences of anti-crime programs and pending legislation. Evaluation studies that examined best practices in the establishment and operation of IOC intelligence-gathering centers would help improve their performance. Others noted that the technologies require evaluation as well, for example, using technology to secure segments of international borders and determining whether such investments were more cost-effective than other, more manpower-intensive methods. Last, numerous participants noted that asset forfeiture programs required more transparency and evaluations to ensure that they were an effective strategy to combat IOC.

Measures of Harm

The EWG also frequently returned to the need for development of better indicators of harm done by IOC. Whereas the emphasis for policymakers is often on economic harm, social and public health indicators are among some of the other forms of harm that participants noted were important for researchers to explore. One participant related that the national health system of a country only sets aside a small number of intensive-care beds for emergencies or serious surgical cases. If an emergency case arises from a shooting and requires hospitalization, this often displaces an innocent person from access to these beds. Thus, the health service examined the true cost of this scenario and found that a shooting victim costs 16 times more than a conventional patient. When an innocent person was displaced, this further increased the cost and added the additional harm to community safety. Another participant noted that the insurance industry in one country spent 45 percent of its income on fraud detection and prevention.

The EWG felt that the way to proceed with studies of harm was to bring researchers, policymakers and practitioners together to share what is known about criminal activity and harm in a step-by-step process. The starting point might be to take information from closed IOC cases—investigator notes, court records, pre-sentence reports, and so on—and then interview those involved in the cases for more information. Next, the researchers should identify key indicators of harm in these cases, such as money stolen, and use case information such as insurance claims or the costs of private security as measures of these indicators. After aggregating all of these data, the studies should produce better estimates of harm. Some participants noted that, throughout the process, researchers should carefully triangulate sources of information to remove bias or inaccurate reporting.

The group also noted some potential pitfalls for evaluation studies of IOC. The process will require that law enforcement and researchers trust one another in order to obtain access to the information that law enforcement controls. Researchers will also need total access to quantify the data and work with law enforcement and policymakers to clarify the data and findings. Old investigative files are, by nature, biased toward the past and may contain only information that can be proven in court as opposed to providing the full picture of the crime. None of these limitations suggest that the proposed evaluation studies could not proceed forward.

Conclusion: The Way Forward

Overall, the working group was a success. This report contains a significant number of suggestions to the research community on how to proceed. It is important that the EWG was able to explore the potential roadblocks in pursuing IOC research and was able to make suggestions on how to move through them. The group proved that researchers and practitioners can come together for a frank discussion of research goals and how to meet them in a constructive way. The additional insight from international researchers and practitioners also proved valuable, lending further validation to the call for comparative studies in multiple countries.

Although the sessions are a challenge to summarize, a few themes arose throughout the many discussions. The first theme was the developing state of research in IOC. In many of the areas that this EWG examined, the state of knowledge on IOC has developed to the point that researchers can proceed to conduct more advanced studies. The group agreed that larger, more theoretical studies would drive more significant recommendations for both practitioners and fellow researchers and that this is a goal that the community should adopt.

The second theme from the meeting was the need for international or comparative research on IOC. Many participants agreed that studies should analyze their findings in an international context, exploring how studies conducted in one country might still apply to other countries. Conducting such analyses will produce more far-reaching conclusions about IOC than studies relying on dense descriptions of localized phenomena. Although participants agreed that localized or national studies of IOC are helpful, the working group as a whole stressed much more strongly that comparative studies of IOC need to reach meaningful conclusions for practitioners.

A third theme was the importance of researcher–practitioner collaboration to produce good research. On numerous occasions, participants noted that practitioners needed to embrace research and especially the data requirements of researchers. The group often noted the benefits that practitioners derive from research and the numerous times that practitioners have relied on research to form policy or enact programs. Continuing to bring together practitioners and researchers into a mutually supportive relationship, focused mainly on data and analysis, will only improve the research and the recommendations it can make to practitioners.

A fourth theme was the need for interdisciplinary studies of IOC. Currently, criminologists dominate the field of IOC research. However, the group noted contributions from other fields, such as political science, economics and history, that have significant impact on our understanding of IOC. Some participants noted that researchers from business schools could provide another useful voice in IOC research. Indeed, one participant noted that the Harvard Business School conducted a study of the black market in Europe. By using an interdisciplinary approach to IOC research, studies can expand to include a more diverse set of research methods and data sources. In the absence of quantifiable data, for example, researchers need to engage in ethnographic methods in order to produce results. Moreover, whereas scholars often view the word "anecdotal" as a negative term, studies based on anecdotal evidence are not necessarily poor but rather are limited in the breadth of conclusions they can make.

The last theme was concern for the IOC research community. Although it is outside the scope of the EWG, many participants noted that the numerous research agendas presented at the meeting would require not just a sustained effort on the part of research sponsors but also a robust research community to undertake and continue the studies. On numerous occasions, the group acknowledged the need for more focused efforts on encouraging graduate students and junior faculty to study IOC. The group recommended that this was a topic worth exploring in more detail in a future meeting of experts.

In conclusion, the EWG provided a few concrete suggestions on how to ensure progress in research on IOC. First is for the IOC research community to take on the larger questions of social science, such as state building and crime prevention. In so doing, IOC research would gain credibility where it does not already exist as well as attracting more scholars to the field. Such a move would also force research to engage in more sophisticated and theoretical designs that could yield more scientific results. In summary, taking on larger research agendas would move IOC closer to the central drivers of social science research.

Second, a permanent mechanism between researchers and stakeholders is needed. Too often, the group noted, as research into IOC has unfolded in one or more of these areas, stakeholders had lost interest in the findings until they realized that they needed researchers' assistance, even for more short-term research outcomes. By creating a permanent link between stakeholders and researchers, information can flow more readily to stakeholders, and the critical feedback on the practicality of research can flow back to scholars. Such a link is especially important when scholars have "bad news" to relay to stakeholders, such as evaluations proving that programs are ineffective.

In the end, the state of knowledge of IOC is advancing but uneven, growing in some areas but just beginning in others. Obstacles and barriers remain, but paths forward and possible solutions are beginning to emerge. Serious questions remain about the power of research, but equally serious requirements from stakeholders suggest that research on IOC will find its way into the central decision-making processes of stakeholders. Through its work, the EWG was able to provide the baseline from which future IOC research can grow.

APPENDIX A: AGENDA

Thursday, January 28, 2010

8:00 a.m.	**Registration and Networking Coffee**
8:30 a.m.	**Greetings and Welcome** ▶ Laurie Robinson, Assistant Attorney General, U.S. Department of Justice ▶ Kristina Rose, Acting Director, National Institute of Justice
8:45 a.m.	**Opening Remarks** David W. Ogden, Deputy Attorney General, U.S. Department of Justice
9:00 a.m.	**Introductions and Charge for the Group** John T. Picarelli, National Institute of Justice
9:15 a.m.	**The National Intelligence Estimate on International Organized Crime** Mathew J. Burrows, National Intelligence Council
9:30 a.m.	**Stakeholder Panel** What gaps in our knowledge of international organized crime most concern U.S. government agencies? How can the research of academic and other private sector institutions have the maximum impact on U.S. policy and practice? ***Panelists:*** ▶ Jennifer Shasky Calvery, U.S. Department of Justice ▶ Robert Werner, U.S. Department of the Treasury ▶ Derek Benner, U.S. Department of Homeland Security ▶ David Luna, U.S. State Department
10:30 a.m.	**Break**
11:00 a.m.	**Actors** How diversified are the criminal activities of international criminal organizations? To what degree are crime groups forming for the sole purpose of facilitating single forms of crime (e.g., document fraud)? How do other actors, especially legitimate or seemingly legitimate actors, facilitate and otherwise participate in international organized crime? How do international criminal organizations learn? How do they communicate with one another? How do they recruit? ***Facilitators:*** ▶ Jay Albanese, Virginia Commonwealth University ▶ Klaus von Lampe, John Jay College of Criminal Justice

12:30 p.m.	**Lunch:** ***Speaker:***	**Legal Racketeering in Russia** Thomas Firestone Resident Legal Advisor U.S. Embassy — Moscow

2:00 p.m. **National Security Issues**

How are international criminal organizations attempting to co-opt the state to suit its interests? How are states attempting to use international criminal organizations to advance their interests? How does international organized crime present itself as a national security threat to different types of countries? How do links to other malevolent actors, like terrorist or insurgent groups, manifest themselves and factor into the previous questions?

Facilitators:

- Phil Williams, University of Pittsburgh
- Vanda Felbab-Brown, The Brookings Institution
- Bruce Ohr, U.S. Department of Justice

3:30 p.m. **Break**

4:00 p.m. **Smuggling Patterns**

How do different forms of smuggling operate? What drives similarities and differences between smuggling enterprises? What are the causes of smuggling patterns?

Facilitators:

- Peter Andreas, Brown University
- H. Richard Friman, Marquette University
- Derek Benner, Immigration and Customs Enforcement

5:30 p.m. **Wrap Up and Adjourn**

Friday, January 29, 2010

8:00 a.m. **Networking Coffee**

8:30 a.m. **Piracy and Cybercrime**

To what degree are international criminal organizations involved in the piracy of intellectual property, goods and other products? How are computers and information networks utilized to facilitate piracy and other forms of international organized crime? To what degree do international criminal organizations engage in online forms of crime? What level of harm does international organized crime inflict on businesses and society from these activities?

Facilitators:

- ►Tom Kellermann, Core Security Technologies
- ►Tom Vender Beken, Ghent University
- ►Andrea Sharrin, U.S. Department of Justice

10:00 a.m. **Break**

10:15 a.m. **Penetration of Economic Sectors and Critical Infrastructures**

Are international criminal organizations purchasing business ventures and penetrating financial markets? What investments are international criminal organizations making in critical infrastructures (e.g., rail, pipeline) or strategic materials (e.g., oil, metals)? Can we quantify the harm international organized crime inflicts on these economic sectors? How can we better prevent, deter or detect such interplay between underworld and upperworld?

Facilitators:

- ►Ernesto Savona, Transcrime
- ►Glenn Simpson, International Assessment and Strategy Center
- ►Robert Werner, U.S. Department of the Treasury

11:45 p.m. **Break**

12:00 p.m. **Corruption**

What work is being done on the corruption patterns associated with international organized crime? To what degree is international organized crime driving as opposed to responding to corruption? To what degree is corruption facilitating international organized crime? What forms of corruption are most prevalent when looking through the lens of international organized crime?

Facilitators:

- ►John Heilbrunn, Colorado School of Mines
- ►Louise Shelley, George Mason University
- ►Thomas Firestone, U.S. Embassy — Moscow

1:30 p.m. **Wrap Up and Adjourn**

Appendix B: List of Participants

Jay Albanese Professor
L. Douglas Wilder School of Government and Public Affairs
Virginia Commonwealth University Richmond, VA

Peter Andreas
Associate Professor
Watson Institute for International Studies Brown University
Providence, RI

Derek Benner
Acting Deputy Assistant Director
Financial, Narcotics and Public Safety Division
Office of Investigations
Immigration and Customs Enforcement
U.S. Department of Homeland Security Washington, DC

Mathew Burrows
Counselor
National Intelligence Council
Office of the Director of National Intelligence Washington, DC

Chris Corpora
Senior Advisor (Contractor) Directorate of Intelligence
Federal Bureau of Investigation Washington, DC

Douglas Farah
President
IBI Consultants
Takoma Park, MD

Vanda Felbab-Brown
Fellow
The Brookings Institution
Washington, DC

James Finckenauer
Professor
School of Criminal Justice Rutgers University
Newark, NJ

Tom Firestone
Resident Legal Advisor
U.S. Embassy in Moscow
Moscow, Russia

H. Richard Friman
Professor
Department of Political Science Marquette University
Milwaukee, WI

Mark Galeotti
Academic Chair
Center for Global Affairs
New York University
New York, NY

Greg Gatjanis
Director for Counternarcotics and Counterterrorism
National Security Council
Washington, DC

John Heilbrunn
Associate Professor
Colorado School of Mines Boulder, CO

David Holiday
Senior Program Manager Latin America Program Open Society Institute
Washngton, DC

Lisa Holtyn
Senior Intelligence Advisor
Organized Crime and Racketeering Section
Criminal Division
U.S. Department of Justice
Washington, DC

Tom Kellermann
Vice President of Security Awareness and
Strategic Partnerships
Core Security Technologies
Washington, DC

Michael Levi
Professor
School of Social Sciences Cardiff University
Cardiff, Wales

Nick Lewis
Serious Organised Crime Agency
British Embassy to the United States
Washington, DC

Don Loree
Director
Centre for Criminal Intelligence Research and Innovation
Criminal Intelligence Program
Royal Canadian Mounted Police
Ottawa, Ontario, Canada

David Luna
Director
Anti-Crime Programs Division
Bureau of International Narcotics and Law Enforcement Affairs
U.S. Department of State
Washington, DC

Bruce Ohr
Chief
Organized Crime and Racketeering Section Criminal Division
U.S. Department of Justice
Washington, DC

Nellie Ohr
Researcher
Open Source Works Washington, DC

John T. Picarelli
Social Science Analyst International Center
National Institute of Justice
U.S. Department of Justice Washington, DC

Eric Ratner
Senior Analyst
Crime and Narcotics Center Washington, DC

Peter Reuter
Professor
School of Public Affairs
University of Maryland
College Park, MD

Ernesto Savona
Director
Transcrime Center
Catholic University of the Sacred Heart
Milan, Italy

Ellen Scrivner
Deputy Director
National Institute of Justice
U.S. Department of Justice
Washington, DC

Adam Seigfried
Unit Chief
Organized Crime Intelligence Unit
Directorate of Intelligence
Federal Bureau of Investigations
Washington, DC

Andrea Sharrin
Deputy Chief
Computer Crime and Intellectual Property
Section
Criminal Division
U.S. Department of Justice
Washington, DC

Jennifer Shasky Calvery
Senior Counsel
Office of the Deputy Attorney General
U.S. Department of Justice
Washington, DC

Louise Shelley
Director
Terrorism, Transnational Crime and Corruption Center
George Mason University
Arlington, VA

Glenn Simpson
Senior Fellow
International Assessment and Strategy Center
Alexandria, VA

Tom Vander Beken
Director
Institute for International Research on
Criminal Policy Ghent University Ghent, Belgium

Klaus von Lampe
Assistant Professor
John Jay College of Criminal Justice City University of New York
New York, NY

John Unsworth
Senior Intelligence Analyst
National Police Improvement Agency London,
United Kingdom
Robert W. Werner
Senior Counselor to the Under Secretary
Office of Terrorism and Financial Intelligence
U.S. Department of the Treasury
Washington, DC

Phil Williams
Director
Matthew B. Ridgway Center for International
Security Studies
University of Pittsburgh
Pittsburgh, PA

Edwin Zedlewski
Chief
International Center
National Institute of Justice
U.S. Department of Justice
Washington, DC

Sheldon Zhang
Professor
Department of Sociology
San Diego State University
San Diego, CA

In: Organized Crime
Editor: Jason D. Camilleri

ISBN: 978-1-61324-012-0

Chapter 4

Overview of the Law Enforcement Strategy to Combat International Organized Crime*

United States Department of Justice

In recent years, international organized crime has expanded considerably in presence, sophistication and significance – and it now threatens many aspects of how Americans live, work and do business. International organized crime promotes corruption, violence and other illegal activities, jeopardizes our border security, and causes human misery. It undermines the integrity of our banking and financial systems, commodities and securities markets, and our cyberspace. In short, international organized crime is a national security problem that demands a strategic, targeted and concerted U.S. Government response.

The Law Enforcement Strategy to Combat International Organized Crime establishes an investigation and prosecution framework that emphasizes four priority areas of action against international organized crime:

- **Marshal information and intelligence:** Collect, synthesize and timely disseminate the best available information and intelligence from multiple sources - - including law enforcement, the intelligence

* This is an edited, reformatted and augmented version of a U.S. Department of Justice publication, dated APRIL 2008.

community, foreign partners and the private sector -- to optimize law enforcement's ability to identify, assess and draw connections among nationally-significant IOC threats;
- **Prioritize and target the most significant ioc threats:** Select and target for high-impact law enforcement action the international organized crime figures and organizations that pose the greatest threat to the United States, and ensure the national coordination of investigations and prosecutions involving these targets;
- **Attack from all angles:** Employ all available law enforcement and non-law enforcement tools – including drawing upon the unique expertise of every participating U.S. law enforcement agency in domestic operations, partnering with foreign counterparts to pursue cases at home and abroad, and employing U.S. government sanctions and advisories – all in a crosscutting effort to disrupt IOC activity; and
- **Enterprise theory:** Develop aggressive strategies for dismantling entire criminal organizations, especially their leadership, by using proactive investigative techniques and multi-layered prosecutions.

This strategy is itself the product of sustained cooperation among: the Organized Crime and Racketeering Section of DOJ's Criminal Division, in collaboration with other sections of the Criminal Division; the Federal Bureau of Investigation (FBI); U.S. Immigration and Customs Enforcement (ICE); the Internal Revenue Service; the Postal Inspection Service; the Secret Service; the Drug Enforcement Administration; the Bureau of Alcohol, Tobacco, Firearms and Explosives; the Bureau of Diplomatic Security; the Department of Labor/Office of the Inspector General; components of the State Department, the Treasury Department, and the intelligence community.

INTERNATIONAL ORGANIZED CRIME DEFINED

For purposes of the strategy, "international organized crime" refers to those self-perpetuating associations of individuals who operate internationally for the purpose of obtaining power, influence, monetary and/or commercial gains, wholly or in part by illegal means, while protecting their activities through a pattern of corruption and/or violence. There is no single structure under which international organized criminals operate; they vary from hierarchies to clans, networks and cells, and may evolve to other structures. The crimes they commit also vary. International organized criminals act conspiratorially in their criminal activities and possess certain characteristics which may include, but are not limited to:

a. In at least part of their activities they commit violence or other acts which are likely to intimidate, or make actual or implicit threats to do so;
b. They exploit differences between countries to further their objectives, enriching their organization, expanding its power, and/or avoiding detection and apprehension;
c. They attempt to gain influence in government, politics and commerce through corrupt as well as legitimate means;
d. They have economic gain as their primary goal, not only from patently illegal activities but also from investment in legitimate business; and
e. They attempt to insulate both their leadership and membership from detection, sanction, and/or prosecution through their organizational structure.

While this definition may be read broadly to include international drug trafficking organizations and international street gangs engaged in criminal activity, those groups are not the focus of the strategy. The strategy places its highest priority on those IOC groups that threaten the national security of the United States, the stability of the U.S. economy, and/or the integrity of government institutions, infrastructure or systems in the United States.

The Strategic Threats Posed by International Organized Crime

International organized crime poses eight strategic threats. For the purposes of this summary, examples of these threats are set out below, drawn from published reports, publicly indicted cases and publicly available information from law enforcement partners. Due to the necessity of referencing only public, non-sensitive information, this summary contains historical information (albeit some quite recent), since most of the evidence of ongoing threats – and our law enforcement response – is law enforcement sensitive or classified for operational and/or national security reasons.

THREAT 1: International Organized Criminals Have Penetrated the Energy and Other Strategic Sectors of the Economy

International organized criminals and their associates control significant positions in the global energy and strategic materials markets that are vital to U.S. national security interests. They are now expanding their holdings in the U.S. strategic materials sector. Their activities tend to corrupt the normal workings of these markets and have a destabilizing effect on U.S. geopolitical interests.

One of the most frequently reported examples involves Semion Mogilevich and several members of his criminal organization who were charged in 2003 in the Eastern District of Pennsylvania in a 45-count racketeering indictment for their involvement in a sophisticated securities fraud and money laundering scheme. Published reports state that since that indictment and being placed on the FBI most-wanted list, Mogilevich has continued to expand his criminal empire, to the point where he is said to exert influence over large portions of the natural gas industry in parts of the former Soviet Union. Many commentators have noted the significant role that area of the world plays in global energy markets. Mogilevich was arrested by Russian police on tax charges in January 2008. Other members of his organization remain at large.

THREAT 2: International Organized Criminals Provide Logistical and Other Support to Terrorists, Foreign Intelligence Services and Governments

Each of these groups is either targeting the United States or otherwise acting in a manner adverse to U.S. interests.

International organized criminals have repeatedly demonstrated their willingness to provide logistical support to terrorists.

Viktor Bout, an international arms trafficker, was charged in March 2008 with conspiring to sell millions of dollars worth of weapons to the Revolutionary Armed Forces of Colombia (FARC), a U.S. State Department-designated foreign terrorist organization. Along with an accomplice, Bout allegedly agreed to sell 100 surface-to-air missiles to the FARC, as well as launchers for armor-piercing rockets. Unbeknownst to Bout, the people he believed to be FARC members were actually confidential sources working with the Department of Justice. Viktor Bout is being held in Thailand on a provisional arrest warrant and complaint issued out of the Southern District of New York. The Department of Justice is currently seeking Bout's extradition from Thailand, where he is being held, to face trial in the United States.

Likewise, an ICE undercover investigation revealed an Indonesian smuggling ring that, in 2006, conspired to export state-of-the-art firearms, machine guns and ammunition, surface-to-air missiles, night vision goggles and other military weapons from the United States to the Liberation Tigers of Tamil Eelam (Tamil Tigers) operating within Sri Lanka, to be used to fight against Sri Lankan government forces. The Tamil Tigers, a U.S. State Department-designated foreign terrorist organization, has advocated the violent overthrow of the Sri Lankan government, employing acts of violence, including suicide bombings, against both civilian and military targets. In this case, the conspirators contacted an undercover business located in Maryland about the sale of military weapons. Six members of the international smuggling ring, Thirunavukarasu Varatharasa, Haji Subandi, Haniffa Osman, Erick Wotulo, Reinhard Rusli, and Helmi Soedirdja have pleaded guilty in United States District Court in the District of Maryland.

A number of published works on organized crime point out that, historically, governments and their intelligence and security services have used organized criminals to further their ends. It is not surprising then that such relationships continue today, particularly in locations where lines between organized crime and the intelligence/security services are often blurred.

THREAT 3: International Organized Criminals Smuggle/ Traffic People and Contraband Goods into the United States

Smuggling/trafficking activities seriously compromise U.S. border security and at times national security. Smuggling of contraband/counterfeit goods costs U.S. businesses billions of dollars annually, and the smuggling/trafficking of people leads to exploitation that threatens the health and lives of human beings.

Whether smuggling people or goods, international organized crime groups view borders as profit-making opportunities rather than obstacles. Whether they are transporting human beings, narcotics, pharmaceuticals, cigarettes or weaponry, sophisticated criminal networks are adept at exploiting gaps and weaknesses in border controls and finding opportunities for corruption.

In February 2008, five members of an alien smuggling organization were sentenced for their roles in a conspiracy to smuggle purported terrorists to the United States from Colombia. Victor Daniel Salamanca, Jalal Sadat Moheisena and Carmen Maria Ponton Caro were sentenced to 70 months in prison after pleading guilty to conspiracy to provide material support or resources to the FARC. Their co-conspirators Nicolas Ricardo Tapasco Romero and Edizon Ramirez Gamboa were sentenced to three years incarceration after pleading guilty to conspiracy to commit alien smuggling and bringing aliens to the United States for private financial gain. The international smugglers obtained fraudulent Colombian and Spanish passports and other identity documents for people they believed to be terrorists seeking illicit travel to Miami for the purposes of laundering FARC money from the United States to Colombia. In fact, the purported terrorists were informants working in an ICE sting operation.

In March 2006, one of the most successful alien smugglers of all time, Cheng Chui Ping, better known as "Sister Ping," was sentenced to 35 years in prison for her role in leading an international alien smuggling organization. She smuggled more than 1000 aliens into the United States during the course of her career, sometimes hundreds at a time, and her actions exemplify the threats to health and life inherent to the trade. The trial revealed one incident in which 14 aliens died when one of her smuggling boats capsized. In another notorious incident, 10 aliens drowned when the Golden Venture, a smuggling ship Sister Ping helped finance for several other alien smugglers, intentionally grounded off the coast of Queens, N.Y., in June 1993 because the offloading vessel failed to meet it at sea. Sister Ping also hired armed thugs from the Fuk Ching, a vicious gang in New York's Chinatown, to transport her customers and ensure they paid their smuggling fees.

A pair of companion cases – Operation Royal Charm in New Jersey and Operation Smoking Dragon in Los Angeles – exemplifies the economic and public health costs of contraband smuggling. These investigations uncovered an Asian criminal organization that was smuggling nearly every form of contraband imaginable, providing a one-stop-shopping point to its customers. The investigations resulted in the indictment of 87 individuals who were involved in smuggling goods into the ports of Newark, N.J., Los Angeles, and Long Beach, Calif., by using shipping containers with bills of lading that falsely identified the contents as toys and furniture from China. Instead, the smugglers brought in high quality counterfeit U.S. currency that had reportedly been produced in North Korea, as well as contraband from China. The contraband included counterfeit cigarettes, ecstasy, methamphetamine and counterfeit pharmaceuticals. Two of the defendants, in a conversation with federal undercover agents, entered into a deal to provide various weapons, including silenced pistols, rocket launchers, silenced sub-machine guns and automatic rifles.

The Camorra, an Italian organized crime group based in the Campania region of Italy, manufactures designer clothing knock-offs in Italy, then transports some of their material to the United States, where Camorra members retail these wares to U.S. customers. Proceeds filter back to Italian-based Camorra clans. Camorra clans are primarily involved in extortion, infiltration of legitimate businesses, labor racketeering, document forgery, alien smuggling and the sale of counterfeit goods. Press reports indicate that these enterprises earn the Camorra clans roughly $25 billion annually, with counterfeit goods sales representing more than 10 percent of this total. In July 2004, Italian authorities issued approximately 70 arrest warrants targeting a Camorra ring that trafficked in tens of millions of dollars in counterfeit goods, including designer clothing, electronic camera equipment and power tools. The ring operated in many countries outside Italy, including the United States. With assistance from U.S. law enforcement, approximately 300 million euros worth of real property, bank accounts and businesses were seized at the time of the arrests.

THREAT 4: International Organized Criminals Exploit the U.S. and International Financial System to Move Illicit Funds

International organized criminals transfer billions of dollars of illicit funds annually through the U.S. financial system. To continue this practice, they seek to corrupt financial and non-financial intermediaries globally.

Eurasian organized crime groups are a particular concern because of their systemic use of sophisticated schemes to move and conceal their criminal proceeds using U.S. banking institutions and U.S. incorporated shell companies. These groups have mastered techniques to overcome robust anti-money laundering controls and are able to move illicit funds through the formal banking system while disguising the source and ownership of the funds. They offer their illegal financial services for a fee to others who are similarly interested in disguising the sources and ownership of their funds.

The Bank of New York (BNY) case was an early example of such a scheme. In 2000, Peter Berlin, a Russian émigré, and his wife, Lucy Edwards, also a Russian émigré, who was a BNY vice president, pleaded guilty in U.S. District Court for the Southern District of New York to conspiracy to commit money laundering and to operate an unlawful banking and money transmitting business, and to aid and abet Russian banks in conducting unlawful and unlicensed banking activities in the United States. Berlin and Edwards teamed in their illegal scheme with two Moscow-based banks that offered to move money for "clients" without regard to the source or ownership of the funds. During the three and half years Edwards and Berlin were involved in the illegal operation, approximately $7 billion flowed through the BNY accounts they had established to third-party transferees around the world. BNY admitted its anti-money laundering control lapses, entering into a non-prosecution agreement with the U.S. Attorneys' Offices for the Southern and Eastern Districts of New York in November 2005 to resolve two separate criminal investigations. BNY agreed to forfeit $26 million to the United States, and to pay $12 million in restitution to victims of a fraud scheme in the Eastern District case.

Another example is the case of Garri Grigorian, a Russian national living in the United States who helped launder more than $130 million on behalf of the Moscow-based Intellect Bank and its customers, through bank accounts in Sandy, Utah. Grigorian and his co-conspirators set up two U.S. shell companies and then set up multiple bank accounts for those companies in Utah. The companies never did any business; they existed only to create the illusion that transactions to and from their bank accounts were legitimate trade. Once those accounts were set up, Intellect Bank could use them to conduct U.S. dollar wire transfers on behalf of their clients. In total there were more than 5,000 of these wire transfers in a little more than two years. In August 2005, Grigorian was sentenced to 51 months in prison and ordered to pay $17.42 million in restitution to the Russian government.

Criminals have learned from the Bank of New York and Grigorian prosecutions and devised a more complicated version of the same scheme to evade law enforcement. Criminals who establish shell corporations in the United States are now increasingly opening bank accounts for those corporations in offshore jurisdictions where customer identification requirements may be less rigorous. However, these corporations are still able to gain access to the U.S. financial system if the foreign bank has a correspondent account at a U.S. financial institution. On the surface, it appears as though wire transfers are being made to further foreign trade with a

U.S. company that has a bank account in New York. In actuality, the criminals are running a sophisticated money laundering scheme in which it is nearly impossible to determine the source, nature or destination of the money moving through it (which by all estimations amounts to billions of dollars annually).

THREAT 5: International Organized Criminals Use Cyberspace to Target U.S. Victims and Infrastructure

International organized criminals use an endless variety of cyberspace schemes to steal hundreds of millions of dollars at a cost to consumers and the U.S. economy. These schemes also jeopardize the security of personal information, the stability of business and government infrastructures, and the security and solvency of financial investment markets.

One example of the intersection between organized crime and cybercrime is found in Romania. There, traditional Romanian organized crime figures, previously arrested for crimes such as extortion, drug trafficking and human smuggling, are collaborating with other criminals to bring segments of the young hacker community under their control. They organize these new recruits into cells based on their cyber-crime specialty and they routinely target U.S. businesses and citizens in a variety of fraud schemes.

One of the most lucrative schemes involves online auction fraud, where U.S. citizens are tricked into buying or selling goods, and never receive the funds or merchandise. One particular online criminal, using the online nickname "Vladuz" engaged in multiple fraud schemes, including hacking into the computers of eBay, the largest online auction retailer. On April 17, 2008, Vlad Duiculescu, a/k/a "Vladuz" was arrested in Romania by Romanian police officials and charged with crimes related to these schemes. It is believed that Vladuz is a participant in a ring of Romanian hackers who work together to develop joint U.S. targets for online frauds, share hacking techniques and launder proceeds from multiple crimes committed in the United States. U.S. prosecutors and law enforcement agents worked in Romania with Romanian officials to ensure that a case could be successfully prosecuted in Romania.

THREAT 6: International Organized Criminals Are Manipulating Securities Exchanges and Perpetrating Sophisticated Frauds

International organized criminals use fraud to steal from U.S. investors and rob U.S. consumers and government agencies of billions of dollars.

Increasingly, domestic and international securities markets have become ripe sectors for abuse by international organized criminals who seek to enrich themselves from the pockets of unsuspecting investors. Using the fast-paced securities markets, the Internet and the wire services – where money, communications and inducements can be exchanged in milliseconds – international organized criminals manipulate international borders and the limitations in law enforcement's detection capability to their advantage without the need to set up a base of operations in any one location. International organized criminals are also adept at using the Internet, wire services and the mails for sophisticated fraud schemes.

Highly organized groups of overseas scam artists have been preying on North American consumers via the mail or over the Internet, attempting to pass authentic-looking counterfeit business checks or money orders. Victims have been approached after posting items for sale or rent on the Internet, meeting a supposed companion on a social dating website, or via "spam" e-mails sent by the West African criminal groups based in Nigeria, the Netherlands or Canada, announcing the victim has won a prize or can share in a business opportunity. In all the scams, the victim is sent a check for an advance payment of the item being offered, or to pay taxes or fees on the sudden riches. The criminal instructs the victim to wire all or part of the check back overseas. However, it often takes weeks for counterfeits to be discovered and the victim is responsible for what has been wired away. U.S. Postal Inspectors have been working with law enforcement in Nigeria, Canada, the Netherlands and the United Kingdom to stop the counterfeit checks from reaching their victims. Since the global counterfeit initiative targeting these international criminal organizations began in January 2007, 77 arrests have been made and more than 600,000 fake checks valued at over $2.5 billion have been seized.

Telemarketing fraud is yet another means by which international organized criminals fraudulently obtain funding. For example, in Canada, the Royal Canadian Mounted Police have linked the leaders of telemarketing fraud rings operating out of boiler rooms with traditional organized crime groups in Canada. The Canadian anti-fraud call center estimates that 500 to

1,000 criminal telemarketing boiler room operations are conducted on any given day in Canada, grossing about $1 billion a year.

One Montreal-based telemarketing ring, broken up in a U.S.-Canadian joint operation in December 2006, victimized as many as 500 people per week, many of them U.S. citizens. Investigators targeted boiler rooms from which the ring would contact its victims and arrested 40 Canadian citizens on the suspicion of fraud. The criminals used two different telemarketing schemes to swindle unsuspecting victims, netting $8 to 13 million annually. In the first, a lottery scheme, victims were persuaded they had won the lottery, but needed to send check payments ranging from $1,500 to $60,000 to cover various costs. Approximately 90 percent of the victims in this case were more than 60 years old. The second scheme, a mass telemarketing fraud, used several approaches including telling victims they were eligible to receive a $7,000 grant, selling victims health care kits or billing victims for services never rendered. In each instance, victims were told to send money via certified check or money order.

THREAT 7: International Organized Criminals Corrupt and Seek to Corrupt Public Officials in the United States and Abroad

International organized criminals must corrupt public officials to operate and protect their illegal operations, and to increase their sphere of influence. They have been successful in systematically corrupting public officials around the world, including countries of vital strategic importance to the United States, and they are increasingly seeking to influence U.S. officials by legal and illegal means.

In March 2008, the Bulgarian chief directorate for combating organized crime (CDCOC), a branch of the Ministry of Interior, reportedly revealed that several officials from the ministry had had contacts with controversial businessmen, link to international organized crime, who were currently under investigation. As part of the scandal, Ivan Ivanov, deputy head of CDCOC, was charged with leaking confidential information. Ilia Iliev, chief secretary of the Ministry of Interior, was arrested for his responsibility in granting documents to travel within the European Union to a Serbian national with ties to organized crimes.

In some countries, corrupt public figures and organized criminals have attained status, power and wealth far outweighing those of legitimate authorities. In others, corruption occurs as an accepted means of doing business. Corrupt foreign leaders who aid, support and are beholden to organized crime cause substantial harm to their own people and often to U.S. strategic interests. In the most serious instances, the corrupt official him or herself is for all practical purposes the leader of an organized criminal group.

For example, former Ukrainian Prime Minister Pavel Lazarenko defrauded and extorted millions of dollars from his countrymen and ultimately laundered his illicit fortune through U.S. financial institutions. Specifically, in the 1990's, Prime Minister Lazarenko defrauded and extorted $44 million dollars from Ukrainian citizens and proceeded to launder $20 million of these funds through U.S. banks. After fleeing to the United States, Lazarenko was arrested in 2004 and tried in a federal court in San Francisco on money laundering, wire fraud and fraudulent interstate transportation charges. He is currently serving a nine year prison sentence and was fined $10 million by the court.

Similarly, Arnoldo Aleman, his family and other related officials embezzled several million dollars from Nicaragua during his time as president (1997-2002). Nicaragua convicted Aleman of money laundering and theft of government funds. In a related investigation to recover assets at the request of the Nicaraguan government, ICE initiated an investigation into the embezzlement of Nicaraguan government funds. The ensuing investigation led to the seizure of approximately $6 million in assets in the United States, approximately $2.7 million of which was forfeited in U.S. courts and transferred back to Nicaragua during the Bolaños administration to be used for an education program and anti-corruption expenses. Additional funds remain pending in U.S. proceedings.

THREAT 8: International Organized Criminals Use Violence and the Threat of Violence as a Basis for Power

International organized criminals who use violence are a threat to the physical security of the U.S. public, as well as the economic well-being of people and neighborhoods and the ability of law enforcement to investigate their crimes when the threat of violence is used as a tool of coercion. Violent tactics used by international organized criminals outside the United States also threaten U.S. interests when their violence sustains and increases their power to operate globally.

International organized crime and violence are fundamentally connected, such that there is no shortage of examples demonstrating this inherent connection. For example, the August 2007 killing of six Italian men as they left a pizzeria in Duisburg, Germany, has been attributed to the 'Ndrangheta crime syndicate. The killers fired at least 70 shots at the six victims with automatic weapons and then proceeded to shoot each victim once in the head. Published reports claimed the killings were the product of a dispute between two rival 'Ndrangheta clans. According to the FBI, the 'Ndrangheta, based in Calabria, Italy, has about 160 cells with roughly 6,000 members. They have a presence in the United States, primarily in Northeast. 'Ndrangheta specializes in kidnapping and political corruption, but also engages in drug trafficking, murder, bombings, counterfeiting, gambling, frauds, thefts, labor racketeering, loan-sharking and alien smuggling. According to published reports, Italian prosecutors estimate 'Ndrangheta operations at home and abroad are worth approximately $50 billion. Prosecutors say the 'Ndrangheta has set up a network of pizzerias, restaurants and hotels for laundering the group's money.

On March 12, 2007, a federal court in Los Angeles sentenced Iouri Mikhel and Jurijus Kadamovas to death for their role in leading an international criminal organization that abducted and murdered five victims in the United States. Between the summer of 2001 until their arrests on Feb. 19, 2001, Mikhel and Kadamovas targeted wealthy Los Angeles residents who they could abduct and hold hostage for ransom in order to fund their lavish lifestyle. Regardless of whether the ransom money was paid or not, once they confirmed payment of the ransom, Mikhel and Kadamovas brutally murdered each one of their victims by either asphyxiating or strangling them. Then, with the help of their criminal partners, Mikhel and Kadamovas transported the bodies of their victims to the New Melones Reservoir, approximately 400 miles from their base of operations in Los Angeles. Once there, Mikhel and Kadamovas attached weights to their victims' bodies and threw them from one of two bridges spanning the reservoir.

The evidence offered at trial confirmed Mikhel and Kadamovas intended to kill more than the initial five victims. After they killed their last two victims, Mikhel and Kadamovas flew to Colorado to ski and look for new potential victims. They also began planning to send a member of their criminal organization to the east coast to scout potential victims and planned a trip to a yacht show in Florida to search for wealthy Russians who they could kidnap. Kadamovas directly informed one of his co-conspirators that he and Mikhel planned to commit as many additional kidnappings in the future as necessary to amass a fortune of $50 million dollars, intending to kidnap and kill their victims until the bodies they dropped into the New Melones Reservoir were "stacked on top of each other" to the surface of the reservoir. Evidence presented at trial also established Mikhel and Kadamovas' involvement in previous similar homicides committed in Cyprus and Turkey in 2000 and 2001. Adding to the international scope of the group's activities, the money they received from victims moved around the globe in its laundering process, including through the United Arab Emirates, Latvia, Barbados, Jamaica, Switzerland and England.

Keys To Understanding and Responding to International Organized Crime

Several critical factors provide essential context for understanding the threats international organized crime poses to the United States and for developing effective responses to these threats. These key factors include:

- International organized criminals do not need to reside in the United States to engage in criminal activities targeting the United States, its interests and its people. With the advent of globalization, the Internet, international banking and modern technologies, international organized criminals can remain in countries that provide them with safe haven from arrest while perpetrating criminal activities targeting the United States and its people.
- The most powerful international organized crime groups benefit from the symbiotic relationship that their leaders have developed with corrupt public officials and business tycoons. The three elements combine forces to form strategic alliances.
- International organized crime in its highest form is far removed from the streets. These groups are highly sophisticated, have billions of dollars at their disposal, are highly educated, and employ some of the world's best accountants, lawyers, bankers and lobbyists. They go to great lengths to portray themselves as legitimate businessmen and even advocates/benefactors for the local populace and others.
- International organized criminals have evolved toward loose network structures and away from traditional hierarchical structures.
- There are large gaps in our intelligence on various aspects of international organized crime. These gaps jeopardize our ability to

keep pace with international organized crime threats as they emerge and develop.

The IOC threats and key factors summarized above provided the factual foundation for the strategy and served as a catalyst for discussion among federal law enforcement agencies as well as across the broader interagency community on what is needed to combat the IOC problem and how we may effectively integrate law enforcement and non-law enforcement efforts to maximize success.

STRATEGIC GOALS

The strategy consists of nine strategic goals that emphasize programmatic areas cutting across all international organized crime threats. Some goals propose new tools and capabilities needed to combat IOC, while others enhance or improve existing tools and capabilities. Each strategic goal encompasses specific objectives and actions that will enable the Department of Justice and its law enforcement partners to achieve measurable results in combating the threats posed by international organized crime. The strategic goals are summarized below.

GOAL 1: Prioritize and Target International Organized Crime Figures and Organizations for Concerted, High-Impact Law Enforcement Action

In order to most effectively utilize resources, it is essential to formally identify the international organized crime figures and organizations that pose the greatest and most immediate threats to our national interests. Other law enforcement segments within the U.S. government – particularly those combating drug trafficking – have effectively marshalled intelligence and strategically targeted major offenders. Those combating organized crime have experienced similar success over the last half-century in strategically targeting *La Cosa Nostra,* the Italian-American mafia. Each of these targeting programs has clearly identified the threats emanating from their targets and focused law enforcement and prosecutorial resources on the most notorious individuals and organizations. Selecting high-priority IOC targets will be a crucial step toward disrupting their activities and dismantling their organizations.

Key Results:

Establish and lead an interagency committee to select and target the international organized crime figures and organizations that pose the greatest threat to the United States, and ensure the national coordination of investigations and prosecutions involving these targets. This will focus law enforcement, intelligence and other resources on disrupting and dismantling significant IOC operations and lead to the apprehension of high value IOC figures worldwide.

GOAL 2: Pursue Concerted, High-Impact Domestic Law Enforcement Operations Against International Organized Crime Targets

U.S. law enforcement is constantly challenged by highly sophisticated international organized criminals and groups that operate across borders, exploit our economy from within as well as from abroad, and which are always evolving to elude and thwart our efforts to bring them to justice. U.S. law enforcement agencies must therefore work together in cross-cutting, concerted domestic law enforcement operations to attack international organized crime from multiple angles and on a nation-wide basis. This will require every participating U.S. law enforcement agency, from headquarters to the field, to systematically exchange information on IOC targets and emerging threats; combine their unique skills and expertise; and coordinate their resources and capabilities to disrupt and dismantle international criminal organizations. The effect will be to bring the collective weight of U.S. law enforcement to bear against the serious threats international organized crime poses to U.S. national security.

Key Results:

Assemble teams of prosecutors, investigators, and analysts to pursue each IOC target; develop meaningful measures to reward action against IOC and ensure accountability; and undertake initiatives to identify new IOC targets. This will enable U.S. law enforcement to organize and coordinate resources to minimize bureaucratic barriers and maximize impact against IOC targets, and to properly account for the use of resources devoted to international organized crime.

GOAL 3: Team with Foreign Counterparts to Pursue Domestic, Foreign, and Joint Law Enforcement Operations Against International Organized Crime Threats

Every day, law enforcement authorities in the United States and world-wide are engaged in parallel campaigns against international organized crime. Globalization has created a vast new battleground for organized crime that extends beyond national and jurisdictional boundaries. This presents unprecedented challenges to the international law enforcement community. IOC groups increase the scope and depth of their activities exponentially while authorities attempt to navigate international laws and protocols to conduct long-distance investigations. Nations throughout the world recognize the need to cooperate with one another to combat the common threats of IOC. Presently, 137 countries, including the United States, are parties to the United Nations Convention against Transnational Organized Crime. The United States has led efforts with foreign authorities to share information, develop strategies, and conduct joint investigations on IOC matters of mutual interest. Yet, there remains much more to be accomplished. To effectively carry-out cross cutting operations to disrupt and dismantle IOC groups, U.S. law enforcement must capitalize on established relationships with vetted foreign officials and build international partnerships to collaborate in the domestic and foreign prosecution of IOC cases.

Key Results:

Establish operational task forces with foreign counterparts in key locations world-wide to target IOC threats; deploy experienced U.S. prosecutors abroad to coordinate IOC investigations and prosecutions with foreign counterparts; and build the capacity for U.S. law enforcement to collect, translate, and analyze criminal intelligence information on international organized crime from foreign counterparts. This will result in more productive relationships with foreign counterparts and will improve our knowledge and understanding of IOC operations abroad.

GOAL 4: Employ Non-Law Enforcement Measures to Prevent International Organized Criminals from Operating in the United States

In today's global economy, international organized criminals enjoy seemingly endless opportunities for moving, concealing, and investing their ill-gotten wealth through the world's major financial centers. Their market of choice is often the United States, whose banking system, securities and commodities markets, and industrial/commercial assets offer stability, prestige, and global influence. The movement of criminal assets into the U.S. financial system and the investment of these assets in U.S. businesses pose a serious threat to the U.S. economy. There are several non-law enforcement tools the U.S. Government can aggressively utilize to target international organized criminals, freeze their illicit assets, and thwart their ability to use the U.S. banking system and commercial and industrial sectors to advance their criminal purposes. In order for these powerful tools to be employed as a component of U.S. law enforcement's crosscutting efforts to disrupt and dismantle international criminal organizations, however, the law enforcement community must effectively provide their non-law enforcement counterparts with critical information that can be considered and acted upon.

Key Results:

Utilize all available U.S. Government programs, capabilities, and resources to their greatest possible effect to protect the U.S. financial, commercial, and industrial sectors from international organized crime and its illicit assets, and to prevent international organized criminals from entering and operating in the United States. This will ensure that the U.S. Government assertively employs its arsenal of powerful economic, consular, and other non-law enforcement means to target IOC figures and organizations, freeze or seize their assets, and disrupt their ability to exploit U.S. banks, businesses, and strategic assets.

GOAL 5: Collect and Synthesize Critical Information on International Organized Crime Targets for Law Enforcement Action

The ability of U.S. law enforcement to successfully investigate and prosecute targeted international organized crime figures or organizations will depend heavily on the quality of information that is available on the targets and the capability of law enforcement personnel to systematically collect, synthesize, and analyze that information. As international organized criminals cross borders to conduct their illicit operations, U.S. law enforcement must closely coordinate and communicate across agencies and jurisdictions to identify and exchange the best information available on IOC targets so that quick and decisive action can be taken against the targeted individuals or organizations.

Key Results:

Convene an interagency analytical team that will systematically collect, synthesize, and disseminate to headquarters and the field law enforcement and intelligence information on selected IOC targets as well as emerging IOC threats and trends. This will result in a functioning intelligence mechanism that will facilitate critical information sharing among agencies and enable investigators and prosecutors to make connections across jurisdictions to uncover and take action against priority international criminal organizations.

GOAL 6: Develop and Retain Skilled and Knowledgeable Analysts, Investigators, and Prosecutors to Fight International Organized Crime

International organized crime has become increasingly sophisticated in penetrating financial systems, manipulating securities and commodities markets, harnessing cyberspace to perpetrate high-tech crimes, and carrying out numerous other schemes. As they have become more advanced in their criminal operations, international organized crime groups also have adapted to the realities and opportunities of globalization, evolving toward looser organizational structures that are flexible, mobile, and elusive. The U.S. law enforcement community must make every effort to keep pace with international organized crime, by ensuring that domestic law enforcement personnel as well as select foreign counterparts are fully equipped with the specialized skills and knowledge required to effectively investigate and prosecute international organized criminals and to dismantle their organizations.

Key Results:

Hold regular criminal intelligence briefings for U.S. law enforcement to ensure that investigators, prosecutors, and analysts have sufficient and up-to-date knowledge of the most significant IOC threats; develop a training cadre to provide IOC training to domestic and foreign law enforcement personnel in the specialized skills required to combat IOC; promote measures to retain experienced personnel; and develop a reserve group of IOC experts to provide case-specific training and mentoring. This will provide U.S. law enforcement and selected foreign counterparts with specialized skills to combat international criminal organizations, and will ensure continuity in the IOC program.

GOAL 7: Provide Law Enforcement with Updated Legislation and Operational Procedures Needed to Combat International Organized Crime

In today's world of international crime fighting, the categories of "domestic" or "foreign" law enforcement cases are almost archaic. International organized criminals simply do not operate within the confines of national borders and geographic law enforcement jurisdictions. Yet, all too often our criminal laws and operational procedures do not sufficiently equip us to address the modern realities and needs of international crime fighting. United States law enforcement and our foreign counterparts are joined in a global offensive against organized crime. We must consider this problem in that broad context and amend relevant laws to enable us to effectively fight international organized crime domestically and in cooperation with our foreign partners.

Key Results:

Expand, update, or modify U.S. laws, regulations, and procedures in critical areas to enhance investigators' and prosecutors' abilities to take action against IOC figures domestically and abroad, and assist foreign countries in developing legislative frameworks for combating international organized crime. This will enhance the arsenal of tools available to federal law enforcement personnel and their foreign counterparts in their efforts to bring IOC organizations and figures to justice.

GOAL 8: Raise Awareness and Leverage Resources in Combating International Organized Crime through Outreach to Public and Private Institutions

The IOC Threat Assessment illustrates the pervasive nature and widespread impact of organized crime. On a daily basis, organized crime directly and collaterally affects individuals and entities in both the public and private sectors. All segments of American society risk being victimized by organized crime, and all share in the increased costs for goods and services. In response, many public and private institutions have acted unilaterally to minimize the impact of organized crime on their respective businesses. These institutions share interests and objectives parallel to those of law enforcement.

Key Results:

Engage the private sector to raise awareness, form public-private alliances, and gather information on IOC threats, and engage other parts of the U.S. government, as well as state, local, and foreign governments, to promote understanding of international organized crime. This will provide U.S. law enforcement with new avenues for exchanging information and leveraging resources to target international organized crime.

GOAL 9: Reconvene the Attorney General's Organized Crime Council to Provide Direction on Policy and Resources and Ensure Accountability in the International Organized Crime Program

The Attorney General has been in charge of coordinating all federal law enforcement activity against organized crime since a 1968 executive order by President Lyndon Johnson established that authority. Similarly, the Organized Crime Council has existed in various forms since 1970 and has always been charged with establishing priorities and formulating a national unified strategy to combat organized crime. This will be the first time the Organized Crime Council has ever convened to focus on the threat from international organized crime and to develop a responsive strategy to that threat. The Organized Crime Council consists of the Deputy Attorney General, the Assistant Attorney General for the Criminal Division, the Chair of the Attorney General's Advisory Committee and the leaders of nine participating federal law enforcement agencies, which include: FBI; U.S. Drug Enforcement Agency; the Bureau of Alcohol, Tobacco, Firearms and Explosives; U.S. Immigration and Customs Enforcement; U.S. Secret Service; Internal Revenue Service; U.S. Postal Inspection Service; Diplomatic Security and U.S. Department of Labor's Office of the Inspector General.

Key Results:

Reconvene the Attorney General's Organized Crime Council to oversee implementation and dedication of resources dedicated to this strategy, review progress in combating international organized crime, examine options for how best to organize the IOC program, and provide recommendations to the National Security Council on new interagency efforts or capabilities to advance the fight against international organized crime. This will enable the Department to engage the broader federal law enforcement community at the policy level to provide oversight, guidance, and direction to the international organized crime program.

INDEX

#

9

A

B

C

D

E

F

G

H

I

M

N

O

P

Q

R

S

T

U

V

W

Y